Bright, James
Franck, 1832-1920.

Maria Thereša.

DATE DUE

OCT 07 1997			

MARIA THERESA

MARIA THERESA

BY

JAMES FRANCK BRIGHT

BOOKS FOR LIBRARIES PRESS
FREEPORT, NEW YORK

First Published 1897
Reprinted 1971

INTERNATIONAL STANDARD BOOK NUMBER:
0-8369-5761-X

LIBRARY OF CONGRESS CATALOG CARD NUMBER:
71-154145

PRINTED IN THE UNITED STATES OF AMERICA

CONTENTS

CHAPTER I

THE WAR OF THE AUSTRIAN SUCCESSION

1740-1743

CHAPTER II

THE WAR OF THE AUSTRIAN SUCCESSION—*continued*

1743-1745

MARIA THERESA

CONTENTS

CHAPTER VI

CHANGE OF THE SYSTEM OF ALLIANCES—*continued.*

1756–1757

CHAPTER VII

THE SEVEN YEARS' WAR

1757–1760

CHAPTER VIII

THE SEVEN YEARS' WAR—*continued*

1760–1763

CHAPTER IX

CHAPTER X

CHAPTER I

THE WAR OF THE AUSTRIAN SUCCESSION

1740–1743

THERE is an obvious difficulty in speaking of the states-manship of Maria Theresa. The statesmen who have influenced the history of the world have been for the most part either themselves the heads of states, reform-ing kings and conquerors, having the power to enforce their will upon all around them, or men whose superior intelligence has entirely dominated their nominal masters, glad to seek relief from the weight of responsibility which lay on them by leaving in the hands of a sole minister the cares and difficulties of government. Such a position no Austrian statesman in the latter half of the eighteenth century could possibly occupy. In the case of the princes who then filled the Austrian throne there was no chance of such delegation of power. Various though they were in character, the determina-tion to be rulers in fact as well as in name was a marked characteristic of them all. The unbending patriotism of Maria Theresa, the ill-judged vivacity

and doctrinaire energy of her son, the cautious political
wisdom of his successor Leopold, alike rested on a sub-
stratum of self-assertion, which rendered the existence
of an all-powerful minister inconceivable.   Yet it is
impossible to attribute to the ruler alone all the successes and failures of the time.   It is impossible, for
instance, to ignore the influence of such a man as
Kaunitz, who for forty years held unshaken the position
of chief adviser to three such monarchs in all matters
connected with the foreign relations of the country,
who three times begged in vain to be released from his
responsibilities, and who towards the close of his life,
antipathetic as he was in his whole character to his
impulsive and philosophic master, was still treated by
him, and still regarded by all his official colleagues, as
the main support of the State.   It is impossible, also,
to leave out of sight the work of such an adviser as
Haugwitz, whose suggestions admittedly formed the
basis of those domestic reforms without which the ruin
of the House of Austria would have been inevitable.

That the sovereign was a queen renders the difficulty
of discriminating between her action and that of her
advisers still greater.   No woman, especially one so
young, could uphold her own opinion against that of her
advisers.   Again and again we see her yielding her clear
views and high-spirited determinations under the pressure
brought to bear upon her, and with sharp woman's
words of offended pride, and woman's tears at thwarted
hopes, surrendering her will to that of her ministers.

Another difficulty lies in the form of the Austrian
Government, and in the character of much of the history
of the time.   In the case of a man of action such as

Frederick II., we know that he was the spring of all
the measures taken by his Governments, and his great
deeds speak for themselves. In nations where any
form of constitutional government obtains, and where
ministerial responsibility is in any degree recognised,
there is no great difficulty in tracing public events to
their sources. But where there is no publicity, where
advice is secretly tendered, and all that is done is
ostensibly the work of the monarch, no such opportunity
is afforded for estimating the relative share of the
adviser and the advised in the overt and obvious action.

Again, the questions at issue are largely of a diplomatic sort. Diplomacy is in its very nature veiled and
secret; in nine cases out of ten its results are obtained
by compromise. The real objects and desires of those
engaged seldom come clearly to light; it is by inference
rather than by fact that the value of a diplomatist's
work has to be judged.

It is thus only in a somewhat indiscriminate way,
and not without much chance of error, that we can
attribute to the great queen the statesmanship, with its
successes and its failures, which carried Austria through
the critical time following on the death of Charles VI.

It was indeed a critical time, not for Austria alone,
but for Europe in general. From the period of conflict
which had followed the break-up of the systems of the
Middle Ages Europe had emerged in a form which for
the moment seemed likely to be permanent. The
monarchical principle had at all events made good its
position. It had indeed acquired additional strength;
incongruous groupings of territories and their inhabitants
had been formed into kingdoms with no true point of

union except in their ruler. Monarchy had assumed an attitude of proprietorship closely analogous to that of an owner of freehold property. But the spirit of criticism which had acted as a solvent upon the old arrangements of Europe had by no means spent its force. Monarchy itself was upon its trial. Political philosophy had already begun to question the sources of royal power, and in England at all events the right of the nation to a voice in its own affairs had been recognised. It remained to be seen whether the despotic kings of Europe would be compelled, with or without convulsion, to share their power with their subjects, or whether they could justify their position by securing the good government of their people. It was during the last half of the eighteenth century that this question was tried. Before the flood of the French Revolution, which was in its essence only the exaggerated triumph of principles already acknowledged in England, swept resistlessly over Europe, a brief space was allowed for the effort of the crowned heads to show, by wise and sympathetic reforms, that they were worthy of the place they held.

But, while thus the thrones of Europe were filled by reforming monarchs, the external relations of the various states remained the same. The feeling of what we should now call nationality had scarcely as yet found utterance. The politics of Europe still rested on the principle of the balance of power, and that balance was still in a large degree personal. It was a balance of sovereigns rather than of peoples. If the smothered movement towards national life was complicating the position of the sovereign within the limits of his own dominions, the existing system of balance was receiving rude shocks from the forcible introduction of new Powers which would henceforth have to be accounted for.

To all the difficulties of this period Austria was more especially exposed. Nowhere was the want of union so obvious as in the complex dominion of the Austrian House; nowhere had the provinces which formed the Empire so slight a bond between them; nowhere were they so entirely dependent for their national feeling upon the person of their ruler. Again, in no country of Europe, with the exception of Poland, had the worn-out principles of mediæval society so firm a hold; nowhere were the exclusive privileges of the nobility so striking. At the same time, Austria's external relations were complicated more than those of any other country by the intrusive energy of the House of Brandenburg, and overwhelmed by the unknown power of the rising empire of Russia.

To guide an empire, with even partial success, through so dangerous a time required the hand of a statesman of more than ordinary ability. The credit of such success as attended the policy of Austria must be divided between Maria Theresa herself and the circle of able men by whose advice she was assisted, among whom incomparably the most important was Prince Kaunitz.

The close of the reign of Charles VI. had been a time of much disaster. The one absorbing passion of the emperor's life was the continuance of the undivided inheritance of the Austrian House to his own descendants. Without male heirs, he had sought to secure this great object by an Act known as the Pragmatic Sanction, settling the succession on his eldest daughter, Maria Theresa. To procure the acceptance of this settlement, and its guarantee by foreign Powers, had been the governing principle of his policy. For this he had paid high. The close of the war of the Polish succession had been purchased by large concessions; Naples and Sicily had been yielded to the Spanish prince, Don Carlos; a great strip of Lombardy had passed into the hands of the Sardinian king; Lorraine had been surrendered to France, in exchange for the grand duchy of Tuscany; while his dominions had been still further diminished when, at the close of his last war with Turkey, the Treaty of Belgrade had robbed him of much of Servia and Wallachia. His death raised the question whether even this diminished inheritance was to pass unbroken to his daughter, or whether the work of his later life would prove to have been in vain.

The political morality of Europe was at a very low ebb, rendering it doubtful whether the binding force of treaties would be recognised if they militated against the individual interests of the contracting Powers. The accession of an inexperienced princess upon a questionable right afforded an opportunity of aggrandisement at her expense, which was likely to overbalance any conscientious scruples that might be felt by those who had guaranteed her succession. All the princes who thought themselves unjustly excluded by the Pragmatic Sanction saw an opportunity for reasserting their claims. The Elector of Bavaria had indeed of late shown himself friendly, and had even sent assistance to the Austrian armies during the war against Turkey. But it was well known that this conduct had depended upon a plan at that

time under consideration, by which the younger Archduchess Marianne was to be given him in marriage, and
with her a considerable share of the Austrian dominions.
As that prospect had faded from his view, he had resumed his old attitude of antagonism. No firm reliance
could be placed on the Elector of Saxony, though he
was bound by every tie of gratitude to the Imperial
House, who had even confronted the dangers of war for
the purpose of placing him on the throne of Poland.
Elizabeth Farnese, whose restless ambition had dis-
turbed Europe for the last thirty years, still swayed the
policy of Spain, and still longed for further acquisitions
in Italy ; while Charles Emanuel of Sardinia was a
true representative of the House of Savoy in his unscrupulous readiness to adopt any means for the increase
of his dominions.

Yet it was not likely that any of these Powers would
move unless they received the support of France. It
was therefore a matter of grave concern that, while a
favourable answer was received from every other court
to the circular issued on Maria Theresa's accession
claiming the fulfilment of the promises in her favour,
the reply from France was of a hesitating and dilatory
character. The French Government was in fact medi-
tating a somewhat shameful evasion of its engagements.
Though Cardinal Fleury has been frequently credited
with a fervent desire for peace, it cannot be questioned
that a very eager pursuit of the greatness of the Bourbon
House went hand in hand with this desire. Whether
the aged statesman was himself the director of French
policy at this critical time, or whether his infirmities
had induced him to yield to the pressure of younger

men, he had at all events lent a willing ear to the far-reaching plans of Marshal Belleisle. These plans aimed at nothing less than the dismemberment of Austria. To each possible claimant a sop was to be given. Maria Theresa herself was to be satisfied with Hungary and the archduchy of Austria beyond the river Enns. The Imperial throne, left vacant by the death of Charles VI., was to be filled by a Bavarian prince in the tutelage of France, which would thus remain without a rival as the dominant Power on the continent.

The resources of Austria were not in a condition to oppose successfully the threatening danger. The national spirit was at a low ebb. The profuse liberality with which place and money had been lavished by the late emperor upon the higher nobility had failed to arouse in them any strong sense of loyalty. As is the usual fate of undeserved liberality, it had undermined the character of the recipients. Patriotism had given place to the desire of personal and family aggrandisement; the whole class was devoted to the selfish pursuit of private interests. And meanwhile oppressive taxation and the dull injustice of the seigniorial jurisdiction had rendered the commonalty eager for relief. But the reign of a young girl gave little promise that the grasp of the self-seeking aristocracy would be relaxed, and it was to Bavaria rather than to the House of Austria that the hopes of the people were directed. Want of success had marked the last years of the preceding reign, and apart from the low tone of public spirit which it had engendered, had seriously affected the means of resistance left in the young queen's hands; for financial dilapidation had followed in the wake of disastrous war.

The national revenue had fallen to little more than half its nominal amount. Exhausting taxation pressed heavily upon the industry of the country. Both Hungary and the hereditary dominions had been so stripped that it seemed impossible to wring more from them. The army was in no better plight than the finances. Consisting on paper of 160,000 men, it could show but half that number under arms. Small as it was, it was widely scattered. For the purpose of maintaining the cavalry, it had been found necessary to distribute it among the villages of the lowlands, in companies of not more than four or five men. There was great relaxation of discipline among the officers, who were all drawn from the nobility. It had become a constant habit with them to neglect their duties and to live at ease in their own homes. Moreover, the shadow of late defeat lay heavily on the troops.

The character of the central government was not well calculated to counteract this disastrous condition of affairs. All the ministers of the late emperor had been retained in office; and the Conference, or Cabinet by which the political relations of the country were directed, consisted of statesmen full of prejudice and for the most part in extreme old age. They were dominated by their secretary, Bartenstein, whose social rank excluded him from the sacred circle of the higher nobility, but a man full of active life, and gifted with a rare power in the use of words. Unfortunately he was at this time deeply impressed with a blind trust in the good intentions of the French court.

If the resources of Austria were weak, no strength was to be found from the system of alliances with which it was connected. The political arrangement of Europe, which was supposed to be founded on the principle of balance, had gradually drifted into two great parties. The ambitious policy of Louis XIV. and the overweight given to France at the Peace of Westphalia had rendered that country a permanent source of dread to Europe. Circumstances had placed William III. at the head of a combination against it, and the balance of power had degenerated practically into the rivalry of France and England, with their respective allies. Maria Theresa might therefore have expected to find in the Maritime Powers allies on whom she could rely to oppose the designs of France; and along with them, according to old tradition, should have gone Russia and the princes of Northern Germany. But many quarrels, chiefly of a commercial character, had weakened the friendship which should have subsisted between England and Austria. Domestic difficulties, following upon the death of the Czarina Anne, for the instant paralysed the activity of Russia. While the young Frederick of Prussia, bent upon attaining for his country the position of a first-rate Power, was hovering between the two alliances, ready to join with either, as best suited his own designs.

Somewhat unexpectedly, it was from this ambitious and rising Power that the first blow came, and a treacherous wound inflicted which affected the whole tenor of Maria Theresa's life. It has of late years been customary to vindicate the justice of Frederick's attack upon Silesia. But it is hardly possible to read the frank avowal of his own motives with which he has himself furnished us, and still to take as serious the obsolete claims which he put forward as his pretext. He owns that his leading motives were the love of fame, and the desire to rise above the contempt which had, as he thought, attended the policy of neutrality adopted by his father. He looked around to discover the most favourable field on which to display his activity. He had claims upon the duchy of Berg; but its proximity to France and its distance from his own capital threw doubts upon the probability of his success in that direction. The duchy was, moreover, so small that its possession would add but little grandeur to his House. Moved by these reflections, he turned his thoughts towards Austria, recognised its weakness "with a youthful, inexperienced princess at the head of the Government," and easily came to the conclusion that the appropriation of Silesia, in immediate juxtaposition to his own central dominions, would be the best step he could take to satisfy the cravings of his active love of fame.

The blow was well timed. If wanting in honesty and chivalrous feeling, it was at least the fruit of clear-sighted and practical statesmanship. It was only too plain that he had but to speak the word to let loose upon the head of the devoted queen the whole mass of ill-suppressed hostility which threatened to overwhelm her. Yet Frederick had no particular animosity to Austria and no particular love for France; his views were purely selfish. If his terms were granted, he declared himself ready to devote his whole strength to the maintenance of the security of the remaining dominions of Austria, and to use his influence in placing the Imperial crown, which the queen could not herself wear, on the head of her husband, Francis of Lorraine. There was a cold-blooded calculation, based upon her helpless condition, in this method of action, which seems to have affected the young queen far more bitterly than a more frank and open hostility would have done. During her whole life she never could forgive the man who had taken so unhandsome an advantage of her weakness, neither could she ever forget the loss to which he had subjected her.

Political calculations have seldom proved more false than those which were based upon the personal weakness of the young queen. Never was a sovereign more determined to uphold her rights, or more capable of breathing energy into a dispirited people. Any yielding which was visible in the opening of her reign can be attributed to no failure of courage on her part, but only to the pressure of circumstances and to the unwise advice of the old counsellors by whom she was surrounded.

Had she been left to herself, she would have indignantly refused all Frederick's proposals; for she had not yet fully grasped the danger of her position, and still cherished an ill-grounded belief in the honesty of Fleury's professions. In Bartenstein, indeed, she found a counsellor as determined on this point as she was herself. "As well attempt to wash a blackamoor white," he said, "as attempt to improve the King of Prussia." The duty of Austria lay in reducing to its proper dimensions the new Power whose intrusion threatened wholly to annihilate the already slackened bonds of the German Empire. But the less vigorous members of the Conference, and even the queen's husband, believed that concession was her only course, and were constantly pressing their opinion upon her.

Still more important was the line adopted by the English Government. A never-resting jealousy made the eyes of English statesmen keen-sighted in all that regarded the Bourbon House. The warlike preparations carried on upon the French frontier did not escape their notice. Already at war with Spain, they saw that before long it might be necessary to renew the Grand Alliance in order to check the reawakened aggressiveness of the French Bourbons also. It was a fixed principle in the foreign policy of England to maintain a close alliance with Austria, and to support it as the necessary make-weight to French influence in Europe. But to support Austria for its own sake against a Power within the Empire, which if its friendship could be secured would itself form no inconsiderable addition to a European coalition, was quite a different matter. Although, therefore, there was no lack of indignation at the unchivalrous behaviour of the Prussian king, and although the English Government professed itself ready, if necessary, to support in arms the pledges it had given, it called the attention of the young queen to the threatening attitude of France, which seemed to give the lie to Fleury's pacific language, and earnestly pressed upon her the necessity of purchasing, even at a high price, the friendship of Frederick, or if that might not be, at least his neutrality.

With indignant reluctance Maria Theresa began to give ground. But the scanty concessions wrung from her were of no avail. Again and again the English ambassador, Sir Thomas Robinson, undertook the vain

office of negotiator. While he was wringing concessions
from the queen, the arms of Frederick were carrying
all before them, and with every fresh advance his
demands rose, until at length they included the whole of
Lower Silesia and the town of Breslau. To such terms
the queen would not for a moment listen. The
intervention of the English ambassador served only to
foster the seeds of ill-feeling between the old allies, and
to advance a step further the division of interest which
was subsequently to revolutionise the whole system of
European politics; as a means of securing peace it was
quite unavailing. The terms which, after much persuasion, the queen was induced to offer through the
English ambassador were wholly inadequate. They
were unhesitatingly rejected, and Frederick put an end
to all further negotiation by denouncing with a fine
show of indignation "the base attempt to make him
untrue to his allies."

The word "allies" was full of ill-omened meaning; for the threatened danger had now become a
reality; an alliance had been contracted between France
and Prussia. The Prussian victory at Mollwitz (April
10) had removed the last scruple from Fleury's mind.
In the following month he had promised, by the Treaty
of Nymphenburg, to assist the Elector of Bavaria, both
in his candidature for the Imperial crown and in his
claims upon the Austrian succession. It only remained
to complete his negotiations with Prussia. Their
successful issue set the whole machinery in motion.
It seemed as though the great plan of Belleisle was on
the point of being realised. The first step was the
attack on Passau by the Bavarian Elector. While the

bulk of the Austrian army was necessarily employed
in Silesia, no serious opposition could be made to the
advance of the Gallo-Bavarian troops. The road to
Vienna lay open before them.

Her escape from this overwhelming danger is the
crisis of the early history of Maria Theresa. It has
been usually attributed to the sentimental patriotism of
the people of Hungary. It depended more truly on the
complicated relations existing between her various
enemies, combined with her own remarkable ability
and courage, and a personality which exercised an
extraordinary fascination on all who approached her.

The separatist tendencies of the Hungarians had been
a constant source of difficulty and danger. Sensitively
alive to the risk of being absorbed into the general
body of the Austrian State, they had again and again
resisted in arms every effort at centralisation. Of late
years they had indeed shown themselves loyal. They
had accepted the Pragmatic Sanction, and had even
submitted to the viceroyalty of Francis of Lorraine.
But the recollection of past hostilities and the continual
intrigues of the malcontents with the Turkish Porte
had rendered all confidence impossible. From the first
hour of the queen's accession she had recognised the
importance of the support of Hungary, forming as it
did so large a portion of her dominions. She had wisely
attempted to remove all causes of dispute by at once
issuing a letter confirming the liberties of her Hungarian
subjects, and entrusting her interests to John Palffy,
the most popular and influential of their magnates.
This step had been so far successful that the Prussian
invasion of Silesia had been met by warm declarations

of loyalty and expressions of willingness to defend the
Empire in arms.   The wisdom of authorising the
armament of a people so obstinately bent on the pursuit
of their somewhat injurious liberties had seemed
questionable to the Austrian court.   But advantage
was taken of the present wave of loyalty to summon
the Diet, and make preparation for the formal coronation
of the new sovereign.   Gratified by the speedy recognition of their separate position, and softened by the
thought of receiving their young queen, rendered still
more interesting by the recent birth of her first son,
the members of the Diet had entered enthusiastically
on the arrangements for her reception.   The very cry
of welcome with which she was to be greeted was a
matter of enactment.   "Vivat Domina et rex noster,"
was the appointed formula.   Yet they never dreamt
of allowing the coronation to proceed unhedged by its
usual safeguards.   Much discussion and some hard
bargaining had been necessary before the words of the
coronation oath, and the promises to be included in it,
had been agreed upon.

No doubt when the first struggle was over, and the
splendid ceremony was carried out, and the young
queen in her Hungarian dress cantered up the "Hill
of Crowning," and waved the sword of St. Stephen towards the four quarters of the heavens in sign of her
determination to guard and increase the limits of her
kingdom upon all sides, enthusiasm reached a high
pitch.

But no sooner was the ceremony over than the Austrian
Government was again brought face to face with the extreme difficulty of securing the national confidence with-

out making concessions injurious to itself. The amount
of the coronation gift, and the method of raising it ; the
constitution of the Privy Council, and the exclusion of
foreigners from it ; the acceptance of Francis as joint-
governor with the queen, were all in turn the subjects
of violent discussion. More than once it seemed probable
that the Diet would break up before coming to a decision,
and the country be thrown into hopeless disorder. That
no such disaster happened must be attributed to the
wisdom and tact of Maria Theresa herself. She used
to the full the peculiar gift she possessed of attracting
friendship and giving grace even to refusals, and finally
succeeded in removing or silencing further opposition
by a great act of confidence. Summoning to her the
members of both Chambers, in a few burning words she
described the bitterness of her position, and entrusted
herself, her children, and the crown and kingdom to
the tried fidelity of the Hungarians. A burst of enthusiasm followed as, with tears in her eyes, she brought
her address to a close. The hall resounded with the
cry, "Vitam nostram et sanguinem consecramus." The
practical meaning of her speech was that already at a
private meeting with the Hungarian nobles she had
authorised the arming of the people, and throwing aside
the not unreasonable mistrust which her German advisers
felt, had determined to call out the universal levy known
as the "insurrectionary army," which the constitution
allowed in moments of extreme danger. Before the
Diet was dissolved she had secured the two points of
most importance to her,—the acceptance of her husband's
position, and the promise of abundant armed assistance.
Though her success had not been obtained without

C

considerable concessions, for she had granted the whole
charter of Andrew II. with the exception of the clause
which authorised insurrection, yet at all events she had
avoided the pressing demands of the Lower Chamber
for an exclusive Privy Council, and for a government
wholly distinct from that of the other provinces.

Yet, after all, the help obtained from Hungary was
neither so large nor so efficacious as had been expected. The queen found her safety rather in the
errors of her enemies than in her own strength. The
mutual mistrust of the Powers engaged against her
prevented the successful completion of 'their designs.
France dreaded lest the easy triumph of the Bavarian
Elector should induce him to break loose from its
tutelage. Frederick, as he himself tells us, could not
see without misgivings the increase of French influence
in Germany. The Bavarian Elector was afraid to trust
his Saxon allies alone in Bohemia. The opportunity
was allowed to slip, the march on Vienna was checked ;
and the army turned northward towards Prague, while
the Elector himself hastened to Frankfort to secure the
Imperial crown.

To Maria Theresa the election to the vacant throne
was a point second only in importance to the maintenance of the Pragmatic Sanction. As head of the House
of Austria she could not with equanimity see it robbed
of the Imperial dignity which had so long been the
mark of its supremacy in Germany. As a devoted wife
she was eagerly desirous for the election of her husband.
But her father had unfortunately omitted to obtain for
Francis, who in the absence of direct male heirs was
his natural representative, the position of King of the

Romans. Some of the German princes, who saw with
jealousy that the Empire was becoming practically
hereditary, were ready to assert their independence by
the election of an emperor from among themselves.
Their choice fell upon Charles Albert of Bavaria. That
there would be a majority in his favour was a foregone
conclusion. The Saxon Elector had ranged himself
among the enemies of the Austrian House. The neutrality of Hanover which the English king had secured
precluded him from giving his vote for the Austrian
candidate. The Bohemian vote, being disputed between
the Elector of Bavaria, who had received the homage
of the country, and Francis of Lorraine as joint-ruler
with his wife, was entirely suspended. On which side
the weight of Brandenburg would be thrown could not
be doubtful. To crown all, the neighbourhood of the
French armies would alone have settled the question.
The Bavarian prince was elected on February 12, 1742,
under the title of Charles VII.

The title he had gained was somewhat an empty one.
At the very time when he was receiving his crown at
Frankfort, his capital, Munich, was occupied by Austrian
troops. The queen had been forced to yield to necessity,
and had relaxed the grasp which was strangling her by
purchasing from Frederick at Klein Schnellendorf (Oct.
9, 1741) a cessation of hostilities on her surrender of
Lower Silesia. The immediate pressure thus removed,
an opportunity was afforded for a counter-blow against
Bavaria. With only one enemy to meet, and reinforced
by the Hungarian levies, the Austrian troops began to
assert their ascendency, and the moment of supreme
danger was over. Frederick, however, could scarcely

be proud of what was in fact a selfish desertion of his
allies, and he could scarcely hope that if the queen were
successful, he would be allowed to hold in peace the
acquisition he had wrung from her.   The relief Maria
Theresa had obtained at Klein Schnellendorf was therefore in itself but of short duration.   On the pretext
that the secrecy he had demanded from her had been
broken, Frederick without scruple threw his late pledges
to the winds, and renewed the war.   The conditions of
the first struggle were in some sort repeated.   Again
England came forward with advice, half honest and
half selfish.   Again defeat obliged Maria Theresa to
listen to the unwelcome advice, and the Treaty of
Breslau (June 11, 1742) confirmed on more solid
grounds, and with even larger concessions, the truce
of Klein Schnellendorf.

From this time onwards, though with constantly vary-
ing success, the antagonists were fairly matched.   For
the withdrawal of Frederick had given a more simple
character to the war.   The real aim of the English policy,
which had been so distasteful to Maria Theresa, had
been to remove the obstacle which prevented her from
giving a whole-hearted support to their designs for
opposing the renewed activity of France.   Hitherto it
was Frederick, with his false words of friendship and
his acts of bitter hostility, who had chiefly excited the
anger of the queen.   Though there can be no doubt
that she looked forward to the possibility of winning
back at some future time the concessions forced from
her, she now for a while laid aside her hostile feelings,
and turned them, with all the warmth of her character,
against France.   Indeed, France was scarcely less

blameworthy in her eyes than Frederick himself ; for
was it not French interference which had threatened to
rob her of her dominions and had given Frederick his
opportunity ; was it not France which had attempted
the disintegration, not only of Austria, but of the whole
German Empire ? Thus, for the moment, Austria and
England had the same great object in view, and the
House of Bourbon seemed to stand face to face with
the same great European coalition, guided by the same
determined enemies as of old. With such similarity of
view, the queen had good grounds for hoping that
assistance of a more active character than she had yet
received would be given her by England. A change of
ministry in that country gave support to the hope.
Walpole in 1742 had been driven from office, and in the
new ministry the direction of foreign affairs had been
entrusted to Carteret. The old spirit of opposition to
the Bourbons, half lulled by the wise and peaceful
government of Walpole, was called into fresh life by
the new minister, whose interests lay entirely in the
intricacies of continental politics.

The Peace of Breslau had not only restored freedom
of action to Maria Theresa, it had left her enemies in a
perilous position. The tables were indeed completely
turned. Belleisle found himself shut up in Prague, and
virtually severed from all communication with France.
Already in 1742 Fleury had lost confidence, and had
condescended to speak of peace. In a humble letter
he attempted to vindicate his conduct by laying the
blame of the rupture entirely upon Belleisle. His
overtures had been received by the queen with scorn,
and his letter insultingly published to the world. Belle-

isle himself sought safety in negotiation, only to receive
a like bitter lesson. The queen replied to him with
indignant words : " I will grant no capitulation to the
French army. I will receive no proposition, no project
from the cardinal. Let him address himself to my
allies. I am astonished that Belleisle should make any
advances,—he who, by money and promises, excited
almost all the princes of Germany to crush me. . . . I
can prove, by documents in my possession, that the
French endeavoured to excite sedition even in the heart
of my dominions, that they attempted to overturn the
fundamental laws of the Empire, and to set fire to the
four corners of Germany. I will transmit these proofs
to posterity, as a warning to the Empire."

The queen believed that the garrison of Prague was
in her hands. The efforts of a relieving army under
Marshal Maillebois proved ineffectual. Broglie, who
had marched to meet him from Prague, was driven back
into the city. Only the great skill of Belleisle saved the
French from complete disaster. Forcing his way out
with 14,000 men, he succeeded in reaching France, after
a retreat which, though attended with much inevitable
suffering, attracted the admiration of Europe.

The evacuation of Bohemia and the coronation
of the queen at Prague completed her re-establish-
ment in her ancestral dominions. She could now
indeed begin to think of revenge, of securing in
Bavaria some compensation for her Silesian losses, of
perhaps regaining Lorraine, the great French acquisition
of the late Polish war, and even of repossessing herself
of some of the provinces which Austria had lost in
Italy. Her anticipations of assistance from England

had been realised, great subsidies had reached her.   An
army, under Lord Stair, lay in Flanders ready to cross
the Rhine.   English influence had at length roused
Holland to activity ; and English diplomacy had secured
a defensive alliance with Russia.   The campaign was
brilliantly successful.   Her husband's brother, Charles of
Lorraine, cleared Bavaria, and the emperor was forced
to enter into a treaty of neutrality which left her in
possession of his hereditary states.   King George himself joined Lord Stair's army, and the battle of Dettingen
was won.   It is true that it was rather an accident than
a victory, a fortunate escape from a very awkward
position.   None the less its moral effects were great.
Nothing was talked of in Vienna but an instant invasion
and dismemberment of France.   The queen could not
understand the dilatory movements which followed the
victory of Dettingen.   But these high hopes were soon
shattered.   A simple combined movement upon France
became impossible from want of concord among the
generals.   Charles of Lorraine would not hear of placing
himself under King George ; while, in the king's army,
English and German in their jealousy almost came
to blows.   Worse than all, George and his minister
Carteret were busying themselves with all sorts of
diplomatic schemes.

   It has been customary to speak of the chivalrous
conduct of England in affording aid to the oppressed
queen.   Such a vaunt is futile.   The motive of the
English people was hatred of the Bourbons ; the
motive of George and his minister was the safety of
his Hanoverian dominions and the desire to appear
before the world as the arbiter and peacemaker of

Germany. To gain this end, scheme after scheme was suggested. The exchange of Bavaria for the Netherlands, the transference of the Bavarian House into Southern Italy, the cession to the emperor of certain portions of Austria, the secularisation of several bishoprics for the advantage of temporal princes, were all discussed. But none of these schemes appeared to offer the one condition necessary to secure the approval of the queen ; in none was any recompense offered for Silesia. The advantage of Austria did not appear to be considered ; on the contrary, for the sake of strengthening the coalition by the addition of Sardinia, strong pressure was constantly brought to bear upon the queen, to induce her to cede a further portion of her dominions to that encroaching Power. In the midst of all this diplomacy military movements were necessarily slow. It was only after much delay that the English army crossed the Rhine and reached Worms, and there at length the treaty with Sardinia, which had so long stood in the way of decisive action, was concluded on September 2, 1743.

CHAPTER II

THE Treaty of Worms was the last act of a long course of mingled war and negotiation, which ran parallel with the more important events which were occupying Central Europe; for the Italian dominions of the House of Austria lay as open to assault as Bohemia and the archduchy. The assailant in this case was Spain. The claims upon the Austrian succession raised by the Spanish Government were too slight to render their realisation probable; yet they were sufficient to supply a pretext to the king and his turbulent wife Elizabeth for joining in the attack on Maria Theresa. They hoped that amid the general disorder they might secure a permanent settlement in Italy for their son Don Philip, such as they had already secured there for his elder brother Don Carlos.

The key of the peninsula was in the hands of the King of Sardinia. Allied with France and Spain, he could throw open the gates of Lombardy; allied with Austria, his dominions formed a formidable obstacle in

the way of all assailants. To secure his adhesion was
a matter of the first importance both to one side and to
the other. But, like the other princes of his House,
Charles Emanuel was eager to extend his territories, and
was a master of that shifty policy which is almost forced
upon a weak and ambitious state wedged in between
two powerful and hostile neighbours. It was well
understood that his conduct, like that of Frederick of
Prussia, to whom by his position he offers some analogy,
would be guided entirely, not by principle, but by self-
interest. Offers came to him freely from both sides.
He was not long in making up his mind; it was
impossible for him to shut his eyes to the danger of the
advance of the Bourbons, or to doubt the condition of
dependency to which he would be reduced if they
became unquestioned masters of the peninsula. He
was ready to give his assistance to Maria Theresa, but
it must be at his own price. And the price he asked
was very large. For his own safety he required that
Austria should pledge itself to induce England to keep
up a strong squadron in the Mediterranean. To make
good the almost certain loss of Savoy and Nice, he
demanded the payment of large subsidies; but by this
he gained nothing. The increase of his dominions must
be secured by the cession of part of Pavia and the
Milanese, and the marquisate of Finale which would
afford him an opening upon the sea.

These were terms which Maria Theresa could hardly
bring herself to accept. All diminution of the inheritance left her by her father was not only in the last
degree distasteful to her as a sovereign, it touched her
conscience as an honourable woman. To carry out the

Pragmatic Sanction was to her a matter of duty, and
with what face could she demand of others the fulfilment of their promises to maintain undivided the
succession of the Austrian state, if she was herself the
first to dismember it? In respect to the cession
of Finale, her honourable mind felt still more im-
portunate scruples. Finale had been lately sold to the
Genoese. All the conditions of the arrangement had
on their part been properly complied with. She could
not feel at liberty quietly to surrender what was no
longer hers. But she was compelled to bend to
circumstances. Oppressed with the dark cloud of
danger which enveloped her position, she yielded so far
as to make a temporary arrangement with the Sardinian
king, and to secure for the present, at all events, his
co-operation. She did not yield a moment too soon.
The Spanish fleet had succeeded in eluding the vigilance
of the English cruisers, and a Spanish army was already
landed in Italy. With the aid of her new ally, the danger
was surmounted. Charles Emanuel and Marshal Traun
made a successful resistance, and occupied Modena;
and when the English fleet had forced neutrality upon
the Neapolitan king, drove the Spaniards to take refuge
in the States of the Church.

As in Central Europe, so in Italy, the crisis of extreme danger was past. In both cases the effect upon
Maria Theresa was the same. Her ambition arose, and
thoughts of vengeance formed themselves in her mind.
She did not even despair of excluding the Bourbons
entirely from Italy. To realise so vast a plan single-
handed was impossible. The first thing necessary was
to change the temporary arrangement with Sardinia

into a permanent and close alliance. But at once the balancing policy of Charles Emanuel was called into play. The sole supremacy of the Hapsburgs would be as detrimental to his position as the supremacy of the Bourbons. He shrank from the required alliance. Maria Theresa allowed herself to laugh at his fears, and, in words upon which future events throw a somewhat sinister light, averred that never would she unite with the House of Bourbon to assault or injure a third Power.

But Charles Emanuel saw matters in a different light. Indeed the Austrian position was not a strong one. In all bargains the man who is most warmly bent on obtaining the object of discussion is inevitably the weaker. Maria Theresa occupied that weaker position. Even if her own eager wish to carry the war into the south of Italy had been insufficient to drive her to purchase the indispensable support of Sardinia, she had behind her a clamorous ally constantly urging her to conclude the bargain; for England, intent as usual on its anti-Bourbon policy, regarded the accession of Sardinia to the general alliance as a matter of the first importance. If the position of Maria Theresa was weak, that of Charles Emanuel was strong. He was in fact indifferent as to whether the alliance was contracted or not. If the full price was paid, it would suit him well to join his forces to those of Austria. If not, he had taken excellent care to keep open permanently his negotiations with the Bourbons, and could without difficulty pass to their side.

If the eagerness with which the English pressed on Maria Theresa the necessity of completing her alliance with Sardinia weakened her diplomatic position, her

difficulties were still further increased by the condition
which they prescribed, and under which alone the alliance would be acceptable to them. Regarding their
own interests as paramount, and the interests of their
allies as of importance only in so far as they assisted in
their one great object, the destruction of the Bourbon
House, the statesmen of England were determined that
the arrangements with Sardinia must be such as would
satisfy the Prussian king. For the reappearance of
Frederick upon the scene would inevitably compel
Maria Theresa to employ all her resources in with-
standing him, and would render a combined attack on
France impossible. Yet this condition exactly contra-
vened the chief object of the Austrian court, the
acquisition of some compensation for the lost Silesian
provinces. There thus arose a complicated diplomatic
knot which it seemed almost impossible to untie. Even
when Maria Theresa had brought herself to consent to
the cessions required by the Sardinian king, she was
still determined that their completion should depend
upon the success of the alliance and her acquisition of
a recompense for Silesia. Charles Emanuel would listen
to no such conditional arrangement, he insisted that his
acquisitions should be immediate and not dependent
upon the chances of the future ; while the English
would agree to no plan by which Prussia should be
injuriously affected. A deadlock thus seemed to have
been reached. None of the many suggestions offered
found favour, and there appeared no chance that the
negotiations would lead to a treaty. The Sardinian
king began to act unreservedly in his own interests.
He refused to quarrel with the Pope, who had shown

strong Bourbon proclivities. He refused to accept the
opportunity offered by the victory of Campo Santo
(February 3, 1743), where the Spanish general the
Count de Gages had been defeated, and to move south-
ward. Yet when the Austrian court, yielding to the
advancing claims of Sardinia, thought it had arrived at
a solution which might prove acceptable to all parties,
England put a veto upon it. The Austrian troops were
still occupying Bavaria, and it was thought that the
emperor might be induced to exchange his ancestral
dominions from which he was thus excluded, for the hope
of obtaining Tuscany and Naples after the great alliance
had conquered them. Bavaria would thus be the required
remuneration for Silesia, and the German emperor obtain
a fitting settlement. The suggestion was peremptorily
rejected by the English. Not only was it entirely
in the air; but it could not be supposed that Prussia
would quietly submit to such an increase to Austrian
influence as was implied by the possession of Bavaria.

Thus, at once pressed and hindered by her English
allies, Maria Theresa began to consider whether better
terms could not be obtained from her enemies than
from her selfish friends. She bitterly blamed her
advisers for having forced her into hostility with
France. "How much better would it have been," she
said, "to have followed the example of the Sardinian
king, and to have left both doors open." She was
the more inclined to take this view because after
Dettingen the French had actually sought an opening
for negotiating with her, and, as she had afterwards
learnt, had been in earnest in their suggestion. The ties
which bound them to Prussia had been broken by the

king's withdrawal from the war; and the emperor, whose support was now the only business which kept them in Germany, was willing, if his own dominions were restored to him, to join in the reconquest of Silesia. That so fair an opportunity had been missed irritated the queen's feelings still more against her old allies.

The deadlock was at length broken by the action of the Sardinian king. Weary of waiting, he brought matters to a crisis. He made it very clearly understood that unless terms could be speedily arrived at, he would throw himself into the arms of France. In view of such a catastrophe, it was impossible to hesitate longer. In September 1743, therefore, the ministers who were negotiating at the head-quarters of the English army at Worms concluded the weary business, and a treaty between England, Austria, and Sardinia was signed.

The treaty was of course somewhat of a compromise. Very considerable cessions were made to Sardinia, among which, in spite of the queen's conscientious objections, were included such rights as Austria had upon Finale. The three contracting Powers pledged themselves to use their best endeavours to expel the Bourbon House from Italy. The number of troops to be supplied by Sardinia was fixed, and if their efforts succeeded, Naples and some parts of the States of the Church were to fall to the queen, and Sicily to Charles Emanuel. But, in accordance with the determination throughout expressed by Maria Theresa, it was only after the conclusion of the peace that the promised concessions were to be considered as absolute. Though this treaty proved fruitless enough, the negotiations which led to it are important. For they tended to increase the division between Austria and her English allies, which was subsequently to change the face of Europe; and they brought into prominence the idea, which recurred again and again during the reign, of some exchange by which Bavaria should fall into Austrian hands.

If the contracting Powers believed that the new treaty would either secure the objects of Austria in Italy or the objects of England in Germany, they must soon have discovered that their calculations were at fault. Its objects were too palpable to escape the notice of any observant statesman. The hand of England was plainly visible, and the main advantages fell to England. The withdrawal of Austrian troops from Italy which was now possible enabled the coalition to act with full force against France. But though this was so, the substitution of a powerful Sardinian army for the troops which had been withdrawn enabled the war to be carried on in the Austrian interest against the Spaniards with every prospect of a successful result. Both branches of the Bourbon House thus saw themselves threatened by the new treaty. Their common interest bound them at once in a closer connection, which resulted in a convention by which the weaker court was promised French support; while France, well able to stand alone, pledged itself to throw aside the auxiliary position it had hitherto held, and to declare war with England as a principal in the contest. The inevitable result of this change in the conditions of the war was to turn the armies of France against the Low Countries. There alone could be found a natural battleground for an English war; there alone could France, with eyes no longer blinded by the glamour of Belleisle's great

plan, see a prospect of permanent and useful addition
to its dominions.

But it was not the Bourbons alone who thought
themselves threatened by the Treaty of Worms. It
was an open secret that in all the late negotiations a
compensation for Silesia had been sought, and that the
quest had hitherto been in vain. Frederick of Prussia
had, since the battle of Dettingen and the apparent
establishment of the superiority of the Austrian alliance,
felt that an attempt to reconquer Silesia itself was
probable; and, as he read the late treaty, its stipulations were chiefly directed to set the troops of Italy free
to be used for this purpose. Eager to get rid of a
constant source of anxiety, he determined if possible
to settle the whole question of the Austrian succession
and bring the war to a conclusion. He recognised his
inability to stand alone, and therefore sought to renew
those friendly relations with France which he had
broken off by the Peace of Breslau. The French
ministry, now definitely pledged to a great war, were not
so foolish as to allow their wounded pride to stand in
the way of securing so powerful an ally. As a guarantee
of the Westphalian treaties, France became a party to
a union of German princes which was formed under
Frederick's influence, with the avowed object of obliging
Maria Theresa to acknowledge Charles VII. and to
bring the war within the Empire to a close. An attack
by the Prussians on Bohemia was expected to lighten
the pressure of the Austrian troops upon the Rhine
frontier, and the conquered territories would afford
the means of endowing the emperor whose hereditary
dominions still remained in Austrian hands. The error

committed at Worms was soon abundantly apparent.
No successful resistance could be offered in the Low
Countries to the invasion of the French king and
Marshal Saxe, his military adviser.   The Austrian
army, which had been intended to complete the conquest of Bavaria and to occupy Alsace and Lorraine,
was scarcely more successful than that of the allies in
Flanders.   General Traun, whose keen sight perceived
the danger that was brewing in Prussia, shrank from
speedy advance.   The vehement letters of Maria
Theresa failed to move him.   He was superseded by
Prince Charles of Lorraine; but though the new
commander carried out the work entrusted to him,
crossed the Rhine and invaded France, it was only to
find himself compelled to speedy retreat by Frederick's
sudden intervention in the war.

Incomparably more important in the eyes of the queen
than any injury which she could inflict upon the Bourbon
House, was the defence of her hereditary dominions
against the threatened encroachments of the Prussian
king.   In that direction she was successful.   The
masterly movements of Traun cleared Bohemia without
a battle.   Satisfied with obtaining the relief for which
alone they had mingled in German politics, the French
did little or nothing to support their ally.   And when,
early in 1745, the Emperor Charles VII. died, the
ostensible pretext on which the Frankfort union had
been formed disappeared, and the only solid link in the
alliance seemed to be broken.   An opportunity had
come to Maria Theresa of reasserting the old
position of the Austrian House, and of satisfying
at once her Imperial and wifely ambition by securing

the vacant crown for her husband, the Archduke
Francis.

For a moment Prussia and France had occupied a
most commanding position. It appeared now to be
slipping away from them. If they desired to retain
it, and to thwart the threatened triumph of their enemy,
it was necessary for them to secure the election of some
rival candidate; and to find such a candidate was a
matter of no small difficulty. It would have been only
natural to continue to his young son, Maximilian, the
support they had given to Charles VII. But Maximilian's
position was not such as to incline him to play the
ambitious part which had succeeded so ill with his
father. Having been once more driven from Munich,
he broke loose from the influence of Chevigny, the
French minister. He saw that no dependence could
be placed upon his allies, and that he would only be
used as a cat's-paw to further their private interests.
In April, therefore, he entered into negotiations with
Maria Theresa, and by the Treaty of Fuessen received
back his ancestral dominions, promising in exchange
to forego all claims on the possessions of Austria, to
guarantee the Pragmatic Sanction, and to give his vote
at the approaching election according to the queen's
wish.

The Elector of Bavaria being thus removed from the
contest, there was but one other rival candidate possible,
and this was Augustus III., King of Poland, and Elector
of Saxony. There was no unwillingness on his part to
undertake the candidature, but unfortunately some lately-
contracted treaties blocked the way. Neither he nor
his minister, Brühl, was capable of any large policy.

They were infected by the general vice of the time.
To acquire territory was their chief end; to side
with the strongest, their only wisdom. When the
cause of Maria Theresa had seemed hopeless, they
had joined her enemies; when she rose triumphant
in the midst of the dangers which surrounded her,
they entered into close relations of friendship with her.
Only a few days before the death of the emperor,
a quadruple alliance had been contracted at Warsaw
between Saxony, Austria, England, and Holland. On
the one hand, the succession of his son to the Polish
kingdom had been secured to Augustus; on the other
hand, he had pledged himself to defend Bohemia with
30,000 men. He had even gone further. By a separate
arrangement with the queen he had promised to join
in Frederick's destruction, and, in exchange for a not
inconsiderable slice of the Prussian dominions, to aid
her in securing the restoration of Silesia. Thus closely
engaged to the Austrian interest, he could scarcely put
himself prominently forward as the rival of the Archduke
Francis. If he gave no very definite refusal to the
suggestions of France, it was probably only for the
purpose of retaining a good card in his hand in the
diplomatic game that was going forward.

The conduct of Frederick was scarcely more decided.
There was no German prince who in his opinion was
exactly a suitable person to place upon the throne. He
was well aware that the jealousy of the Electors was
too strong to allow of his own election, and it by no
means suited his views that so powerful a neighbour
as the Polish king should receive the great accession
of influence which the Imperial crown would have given

him. He also wished to keep his vote in his hand till
he could turn it to good advantage. To this he was
beginning to see his way. His French alliance had
brought him no assistance. The successes of the last
year in Flanders had taught the French where substantial advantages could most easily be acquired, and
they still retained a bitter remembrance of the sufferings
of the siege of Prague, and the retreat which followed
it. The last campaign, though highly successful, had
neither brought help to Prussia nor forwarded the
designs of the union. The battle of Fontenoy had been
fought and the allies defeated. The threatened expedition of the Young Pretender to England had compelled
the withdrawal of much of the English army, and
fortress after fortress had fallen an easy prey to their
arms. But instead of pushing forward into the heart
of Germany and occupying Frankfort, and thus in all
probability securing the election of their own candidate,
the French, under the Prince de Conti, had fallen back
behind the Rhine, and allowed the commanding position
they had neglected to be taken by the Austrians, with
the Archduke Francis at their head. Frederick had
been left single-handed to continue his war in Silesia,
where, by his own unaided efforts, he had won over the
combined Austrians and Saxons the victory of Hohen
Friedberg. Disgusted with the failure of co-operation
on the part of the French, and wishing only to obtain
security, he was already contemplating a change of
alliance, and had entered into a negotiation with England,
as the readiest method of bringing the war to a conclusion. King George was at the time at Hanover, eagerly
engaged in securing the election of the archduke, and

Frederick felt pretty confident that if he withdrew his opposition, and consented to vote for the Austrian candidate, he would be able to command, as he expressed it, *quelques bons morceaux*, in exchange for his consent. But King George shrank from contracting a separate treaty without the participation of his Austrian ally. Yet it was obvious that for English interests the cessation of the war between Austria and Prussia, which was a permanent obstacle to the employment of the full power of the coalition against France, was necessary. The English king therefore urged upon Maria Theresa, through his minister at Vienna, the advisability, if she wished to retain his friendship, of coming to terms with Prussia. She was wholly unmoved by the arguments of the ambassador. Whatever arrangements might be made, nothing would induce her, she said, to withdraw any of the troops employed in keeping Prussia in check. King George, however, had no time to spare for further persuasions ; his presence in England was clamorously demanded by the threatening aspect of the Jacobite invasion. He was therefore obliged to swallow his dislike to a separate treaty, and on August 26, 1745, concluded with Prussia an agreement known as the Treaty of Hanover, by which the dominions of the contracting Powers were mutually guaranteed, and all opposition on the part of Frederick to the election of the archduke was withdrawn. An armistice of six weeks was allowed for the adhesion of Maria Theresa to the treaty.

The news of this arrangement, which destroyed all hope of the reconquest of Silesia, was received at Vienna with the greatest indignation.

It appeared to the queen that an attempt was being made to force upon her, against her will, the very terms she had before so scornfully rejected. She immediately ordered her generals to pay no attention whatever to the armistice. Frederick found some difficulty in extricating himself from the awkward position in which he was placed by this blank refusal of his terms. In expectation of peace, he had kept his army unemployed in the neighbourhood of Chlum, while his enemies were collecting round him. He found it necessary to withdraw into Silesia; but even in retreat he asserted his superiority by inflicting upon the Austrians, as they ventured to pursue him, a heavy defeat upon the river Sohr (September 20, 1745).

Meanwhile the business of the election had been completed at Frankfort. There was no longer any doubt as to how the question would be settled. When the timorous policy of France allowed the Austrian army to surround and occupy the electoral city, it was certain that the vehement and single-hearted policy of the queen would triumph over the shuffling of the Saxon court and the mercenary and self-seeking course pursued by Frederick. Overawed by the Austrian arms, the electors allowed the validity of the Bohemian vote, which had been excluded at the last election. The Bavarian prince was bound by the Treaty of Fuessen. The Saxon Elector refused to be put forward as a candidate. Frederick contented himself with a protest against an election in opposition, as he declared, to the enactments of the Golden Bull. Without opposition, on October 4, 1745, the archduke was elected emperor, and took the name of Francis I.

It was natural that this success should strengthen the queen in her determination to refuse her adhesion to the Treaty of Hanover. She saw clearly enough that peace was within her grasp. But the election of her husband gave her fresh assurance that her position was now so strong that peace was scarcely an object to be desired. " I know very well," she said to the Venetian ambassador during a fête at Schönbrun, " that I have it in my power to make peace. But I will not do so, nor will I hear any arguments on the point. The King of Prussia only wishes to lull me to sleep, and to attack me again when I least dream of it." Even though England deserted her, she believed that her position with respect to her other allies was tolerably safe. " The King of Sardinia," she said, " knows his interest, and that I could make him pay too dearly for it if he deserted me." The Elector of Saxony she regarded as a friend, though lukewarm and discontented. That he was not hearty in her cause she attributed to the enmity of the Electress. " Nothing would content him," she sarcastically remarked, " unless it were possible that the Electress should be made Empress on the election of the Archduke to the Empire."

How deeply Maria Theresa was wounded by the conduct of England was shown by her approaches to the French court. That she should have followed the example of her rival and have turned from inconvenient friends to avowed but conciliatory enemies, though it excited astonishment at the time, can surprise no one now. Direct approach was scarcely to be thought of, but she found an intermediary in the Saxon court. As she passed through Passau, on her way to Frankfort,

to be present at her husband's coronation, she met the
Saxon envoy to the court of Munich and Count Chotek,
her own representative there, who had already been in
communication on the subject.　She took Chotek into
her carriage, and in a long interview explained to him
that she gave up all idea of invading France, and being
very eager to open relations with that country, was
content that negotiations should be opened either at
Dresden or at Munich.　Meanwhile she proceeded on
her journey to Frankfort.　In spite of the orders of the
Elector-Palatine, who had joined Frederick in his protest
at the late election, she was received enthusiastically
at Heidelberg, and in the midst of a perpetual triumph
reached Frankfort, where all the world expected and
hoped that she herself would also be crowned.　But she
declined the honour.　Her health, for she was expecting
a child, was alleged as the excuse.　The meaner motive
of jealousy has been suggested; much more probably it
was her wifely feeling which kept her away from the
ceremony.　Experience had no doubt taught her that
her husband was not the tower of strength she had
hoped to find him.　She had already learnt how
superior she was to him in every respect.　But her love
remained constant.　She naturally shrank from putting
herself forward, conscious that had she been there herself, she would have of necessity been all in all and her
husband nothing; and she was determined that the day
should be his triumph and not hers.　The mixture
of domestic affection, the part which the wife and
mother played even in her political action, is one of the
characteristics of Maria Theresa which explains the
enthusiasm felt for her.　Though she refused to be

crowned, she had no scruple in showing herself publicly
during the festivities. As her husband came home from
the solemnity, she ran out to meet him, waving her
handkerchief and joining in the applause of the crowd.
We are even told—and the little trait is worth mention-
ing—that she took off her gloves, that the clapping of
her hands might be the better heard.

It was in the midst of the celebrations that the news
of the battle of the Sohr had arrived. In that engagement, Frederick, in full retreat, had suddenly halted,
turned back in his course, and become the assailant.
The light Austrian troops already employed in harass-
ing his march were thus able to fall upon his camp, to
pillage it and to bring off his papers. It was not therefore the news of the battle only, but many of Frederick's
secret documents, which were received. They were a
revelation. His correspondence with George was there,
showing with how little respect her English ally had
disposed of her and her claims, and pledged himself
even to the withdrawal of his subsidies unless she made
peace. There also was much of Frederick's correspondence with France, laying open his double-dealing with
that court. The minister of Bavaria, who was present
at the reading, told the French minister that she wept
with anger as she read it. In the glow of her triumph
and her exasperation she naturally refused to think of
peace. The negotiations with France were continued.
The Saxon minister came to Frankfort, and through
him definite propositions for a change of alliance were
made. The immediate completion of the arrangement
was only prevented by the opposition of D'Argenson,
the French foreign minister, and the tedious delays of

the Austrian chancery. Indeed it is probable that Maria
Theresa herself regarded the negotiations, in their un-
formed condition, chiefly as a diplomatic means of
strengthening a very vigorous piece of military action
which she had already conceived.

When Robinson, the English ambassador, besieged
her with fresh importunities, after her return to Vienna,
and urged upon her the necessity of concentrating her
efforts, he met with a curt and decided refusal. Her
answer, which was in writing, was accompanied by the
text of a new agreement by which the Treaty of
Warsaw was strengthened and Austria still more deeply
pledged to assist Saxony if assaulted by Frederick. At
the same time she pointed out the measures already
taken to fulfil this promise; troops under General
Grün had been withdrawn from the Rhine army and
directed towards Saxony, and the Prince of Lorraine
was moving his army in the same direction. Thus
not only did Maria Theresa refuse to accept the
Treaty of Hanover, but she made it clear that she
was already taking steps exactly opposite to those
pressed upon her by the English. Her answer raised
a well-founded suspicion that she had some fresh
project in view. The Czarina of Russia had been at
length brought to declare that the least assault upon
the dominions of the Saxon Elector would be followed
by the march of 12,000 men to his support. Such a
threat was most disquieting to Frederick, and, it was
supposed, would prevent him from making any forward
movement. The negotiations with France, which had
now got so far that Count Harrach was sent to Dresden
with authority to bring them to a conclusion, allowed the

safe removal of troops from the Rhine; and Maria
Theresa had formed a plan by which two armies should
pass through Saxony from either side and converge
upon the Prussian capital. There was every reason to
suppose that while Frederick was paralysed by the
Russian threat, Austria and Saxony would find the
conquest of his dominions a task not beyond their
strength.

It was unfortunate for the empress that she could
not herself carry out her great and decided views; they
constantly failed by weak execution. The strange
garrulity of the Saxon envoy warned Frederick of his
danger. Calling upon France for help, reminding the
English that they were pledged to produce a peace with
Austria, and pointing out to Russia that the Treaty of
Hanover expressly guaranteed the Saxon dominions, he
concentrated his forces near the Neisse and the Bober,
with every care to exclude from Saxony all information
as to his position. Much to his surprise, the expected
onslaught of his enemies did not take place. For a
change had come over the views of the Czarina, and she
now let it be understood that the sanction she had
given to the attack on Prussia did not extend to the old
possessions of the king, but was confined to his new
acquisitions in Silesia. Had the allies possessed a com-
petent or courageous leader, this arbitrary limitation
of their activity would have been disregarded; for
already the mere threat of armed intervention on the
part of Russia had produced the desired effect of
compelling the king to direct his attention to the
security of his own dominions. But the Austrian
generals were timid and second-rate, and the Saxon

court was the obsequious vassal of Russia. The great
scheme was thrown over. The junction with the Saxon
troops was abandoned; the converging assault upon
Brandenburg was no longer possible; Prince Charles of
Lorraine marched with extreme slowness upon the
eastern line of assault; a skirmish at Henersdorf was
enough to check him, and without a battle he fell back
out of Saxony. Frederick, offering terms to Augustus,
followed up his victory by pushing an army straight
towards Dresden. The Elector fled. A battle outside
the walls placed the Prussians in command of the city,
and the Saxon court no longer made any difficulties in
accepting the Treaty of Hanover.

Meanwhile Count Harrach had arrived at Lobositz,
where Augustus had taken refuge. The object of his
mission had entirely changed. There was no longer
any thought of negotiating a combined movement for
the destruction of the Prussian king; it was with this
victorious monarch himself that arrangements had to be
made. The French Government showed no inclination
to support a hopeless cause. The Elector of Saxony
had been crushed and driven from his capital. England
could be regarded as little better than an enemy. The
complete failure of the intended movement was so
obvious that instructions were given to Harrach to accede
at once to the Treaty of Hanover. This was all that
Frederick required, and the second Silesian war was
brought to an end by the signature of the Treaty of
Dresden on December 25, 1745.

It is difficult to believe that the adhesion of Maria
Theresa to this treaty was as frank and thorough as
that of her rival. Considering her conscientious and

honourable character, it cannot be supposed that she avowed even to herself an intention to throw aside her engagement. But with strange self-deception she cherished an unwavering mistrust of the Prussian king, and what was little less than a determination once again to try conclusions with him. It is not therefore surprising that in the following year she allowed herself to enter into a treaty with Russia and Saxony, which was in fact, and in some respects even in words, directed against Frederick. If he assailed either the Austrian dominions or the dominions of Saxony and Poland, or the dominions of Russia, the *casus foederis* arose, and each party pledged itself at once to place 30,000 troops at the disposal of the assailed monarch. Nay more, the treaty went on to say, in case of such a war arising, this contingent should be doubled. As it is habitual for every party in an international quarrel to consider his enemies the aggressors, any dispute with his neighbours into which Frederick might fall would, to all appearance, let loose the avalanche upon him.

CHAPTER III

It was not only the turn which the affairs of Central Europe had taken, but the ill success of her arms in Italy, which had driven Maria Theresa to conclude the Dresden treaty. For the Treaty of Worms had been as unfortunate in its effects in Italy as in Germany. Maria Theresa's consent to cede Finale to Sardinia had thrown Genoa upon the side of her foes. The removal of the Austrian troops for the purposes of the war with Prussia, which was regarded as the chief advantage of the treaty, had left the Sardinians too weak to maintain the war. The French and Spanish armies had occupied Piacenza and Parma; the Sardinian king had been worsted at Bassignano; and the Spaniards had overrun Lombardy and had crowned Don Philip in Milan. The deepest mistrust reigned between the allies. Charles Emanuel was believed to be in constant communication with the French, and had more than once declared that unless more powerful help reached him from Austria, he should be compelled to accept the offers of the Bourbon House. Maria Theresa's own view was of the most despairing character. "My circumstances in Italy," she told the Venetian ambassador, "grow daily worse; and I fear that they will soon have reached a point where no salvation will be possible. I give up everything there for lost. Though the King of Sardinia promises to remain true to his present alliances,—and, indeed, in so doing he acts for his own advantage, as otherwise he would be the mere plaything of the Bourbons,—I cannot but fear that the sorry plight in which he finds himself will drive him to accept the offers of France and Spain."

Maria Theresa scarcely exaggerated the dangers of the situation. Negotiations between France and Sardinia had actually been set on foot. After the battle of Bassignano, the king had demanded of the French the despatch of a trustworthy minister to bring about an understanding between the two countries. The propositions of France assumed a regular form. First and foremost came the entire expulsion of the House of Austria from Italy, and the division of their territory among the Italian princes. Even Tuscany was to be taken from the emperor, and given to his brother Prince Charles. But more important was a second proposition, which seems to have sprung from the brain of the Marquis d'Argenson. It was nothing less than the exclusion of all foreigners from Italy, and the federation of the various princes under one common council, and with a common national army; a sort of adumbration of the united Italy which has since come into existence. This plan did not at all suit the Sardinian king. It did not require much discrimination to see how poor his

position in such a federation would be, in the presence
of Spanish princes reigning in Naples and Milan, supported by the whole influence of the Bourbon Houses.
He knew well that his independence was less threatened
by the influence of Austria than by that of France.
He was, however, unable to resist the pressure of
circumstances. The fall of the citadel of Alessandria,
which was imminent, would have thrown open to his
enemies the road to Turin. While, therefore, he still
refused to complete the proffered treaty, he felt obliged,
in December 1745, to accept a less explicit preliminary
arrangement. Its stipulations were confined to the
partition of the Austrian territories in Italy between the
King of Sardinia and Don Philip, and to the payment
by France and Spain of subsidies as large as those which
England had hitherto paid.

Fortunately for Austria, the exaggerated demands of
Elizabeth Farnese, who would listen to no arrangement
which did not give Milan to her son Philip as his capital,
postponed the threatened dissolution of the alliance with
Sardinia; and for a second time a crisis of extreme danger
to Austrian influence in Italy was avoided; for in the
following year the tide of victory entirely changed. The
effect of the Treaty of Dresden began to be felt. Freed
from her Prussian war, the empress was able to turn her
attention to Italy with the best results. The French
and Spaniards were defeated in a great battle at
Piacenza, and Lombardy was cleared. The accession
of a new King of Spain, Ferdinand VI. (in August
1746), still further contributed to the supremacy of
Austria, for the masculine vigour of Elizabeth Farnese
was removed. Ferdinand was little less uxorious

E

than his father, but his wife was a Portuguese princess, and more inclined towards friendship with Austria than with France. The French army, left without assistance from Spain, was unable to make head against the Austrian troops, and withdrew behind the Alps. The immediate result was the fall of Genoa. France seemed to lie open to assault, and, assisted by the English squadron, the Austrians pushed across the frontier.

In a war so extended and complicated in its character, the balance of defeat and victory has every opportunity of rectifying itself. Successes in Italy were counterbalanced by a disastrous campaign in the Low Countries. As city after city fell before the victorious advance of Marshal Saxe, there was no room for illusion as to the result. So completely did Kaunitz, who was acting as minister plenipotentiary in the Netherlands, despair of offering any effectual resistance to the flood of French conquests, that he entreated again and again to be recalled. Maria Theresa was already too well aware of his value to grant his request; and when Brussels itself was attacked and taken, he found himself obliged to withdraw to Aix-la-Chapelle, and there watch, without any power of rendering assistance, Antwerp, Mons, Charleroi, and Namur all swept into the conqueror's net; and finally to see Prince Charles, who had sought to revive his lost prestige by undertaking the chief command in the Low Countries, completely beaten at Raucoux. The approach to Maestricht, the last great fortress which closed their path to Holland, was thus thrown open to the French.

The fluctuating character of the war and the widespread and meaningless injury which it caused had naturally given rise to the thought of bringing it to a conclusion. The first attempts proved abortive. Holland, in the hands of the mercantile Republican party, had for some time been endeavouring to effect a reconciliation between France and the Maritime Powers. The English Government now determined to undertake the work directly, and despatched Lord Sandwich as plenipotentiary to Breda, where conferences were to be held. The French minister, D'Argenson, was not ready to forego the great hopes with which his Government had entered upon the war. Believing that the natural enemy of his country was the House of Hapsburg, he had attempted to exclude it from the Italian peninsula, and still cherished the hope of destroying its influence in the north of Germany through the instrumentality of the Prussian king and a federation of the Catholic princes of Germany under French protection. To realise such a plan in presence of plenipotentiaries from all the belligerents he saw to be impossible; he therefore clung tenaciously to the exclusion of the Austrian and Sardinian envoys from the peace conferences. This in itself was almost enough to render them nugatory. The negotiations assumed the character of intrigues, aiming at the separation of allies and the formation of separate treaties. No results were arrived at, and when the French thought it expedient, for the purpose of accelerating the movements of the States-General, to cross the frontier and invade Holland, an outburst of popular indignation overthrew the Republican Government, called William of Orange to occupy the stadtholdership, virtually put an end to the negotiations, and necessitated the continuance of the war.

Another year of checkered successes and defeats was necessary before negotiations could be resumed. Neither in Italy nor in the Netherlands was the campaign of 1747 advantageous to Austria. The combined armies in the Low Countries were placed in the incapable hands of the Duke of Cumberland. Though chiefly supported by English subsidies, it was with difficulty that the requisite number of Austrian troops could be found. So inadequate, indeed, were the forces, that the English Government declined to pay the stipulated subsidies without proof that the Austrian contingent had reached its full number. To this indignity the empress was forci ⁻¹ to submit. While the Duke of Cumberland was hesitating whether to adopt his own views or those of his German colleague Bathyany, the French marched directly upon Maestricht. An attempt to check them exposed Cumberland to a complete defeat at Laufeldt, and the campaign closed with the loss of Bergen - op - Zoom, hitherto regarded as impregnable. In Italy the advance of General Browne had been paralysed by the revolt of Genoa. The Austrians had shown no mercy to the conquered city. In a burst of popular fury the inhabitants had expelled General Botta and his troops. The forces which should have invaded France were now required to reduce the re- volted city. Even this task proved too difficult for them. The approach of a Franco-Spanish army raised the siege.

The time, in fact, had arrived when all parties were desirous of closing the weary war.

As far as France was concerned, the war had entirely lost its meaning. There was no reason for continuing it, other than the blind opposition of Bourbon to Hapsburg,

of France to England. The imposing plan with which
the war had opened had failed at every point. The
Imperial crown, far from being on the head of a nominee
of France, was on the head of its chief enemy. The
Elector of Bavaria, instead of affording the French access
to the heart of the Empire, had taken his own course
regardless of French advice, and was not only in alliance
with Austria, but had actually sent his troops to serve with
the allied army. The Treaty of Dresden had broken the
link which joined France to the rising House of Prussia,
and had removed the only serious opponent to Austria
within the limits of the Empire. With the exception
of Silesia, the price paid for safety from attack in this
direction, the empress reigned unquestioned mistress of
her inheritance. But if there was no cause for war,
there was every reason for peace. The resources of
France were nearly exhausted. The victorious course
of French arms upon land had gone hand in hand with
constant disaster upon sea, and exclusion from foreign
trade left no hope of the restoration of prosperity from
that source.

On the side of England, the reasons for continuing
the war were scarcely more obvious. The object which
has necessarily been before English statesmen in their
great wars had been accomplished. Victory after
victory had annihilated the navy of France. The
efforts of the Jacobites, with such support as they could
derive from France, had proved ineffectual. As far as
the balance of power was concerned, there seemed now
no probability of such exaggeration of French power as
to cause any dangerous dislocation of the system. With
comparatively small losses, the House of Austria still

occupied a predominant position in Europe, and a fresh
Power which had given signs of extraordinary strength
and vitality had arisen in the North. But at the same
time a continuous course of disaster had attended the
English arms in the Low Countries, and it seemed
probable that renewed efforts in that direction would
tend only to the advantage of France. Spain, the other
branch of the Bourbon House, had ceased to be aggressive.
Some comparatively slight advantage, which Austria
might well grant in exchange for the large sums of
money lavished in the course of the war, would satisfy
its claims, and secure to the English the continued
possession of Gibraltar.

With Maria Theresa the case was somewhat different.
She might indeed be well satisfied with having emerged
from a great continental war with power still unim-
paired. In contrast with her plight at the time of her
accession, her position in Europe was one of marvellous
prosperity. Every failure in the designs of France had
been a success for her. Moreover, the appearance of
Prussia upon the scene had entirely changed her attitude
towards the Powers of Europe. It was no longer the
House of Bourbon which she had to dread, but the
domestic enemy within the Empire. For these reasons
she might desire peace, and they had already led her
into negotiations with a view to separate arrangements
with both branches of the Bourbon House. Any dis-
inclination she may have felt for peace rested not on
her position with regard to her declared enemies, but on
the collateral arrangements with her own allies which
would inevitably accompany any pacification. And as
a matter of fact, although the contrary has been asserted,

she was not at all anxious to continue the war. But in the last degree tenacious with respect to the territory she had received from her father, she found it difficult to resign herself to those renunciations which had been requisite to secure support during the course of the war, or which were now demanded by her allies as a means of obtaining a general peace.

Well aware of the high spirit and determined character of the empress, the French, though they had been long indirectly negotiating with her, recognised the necessity, if they desired peace, of separating the allies; of establishing first of all with England the terms on which such a peace should rest, and practically throwing upon their adversary the responsibility of bringing the empress to accede to them. It was an old trick of French diplomacy, and already at the Treaty of Utrecht its employment had sown the seeds of disunion between England and her allies. With this view, the French ministers proposed as the preliminary basis of a general pacification terms so simple that they have been misconstrued as though they originated in a chivalrous love of justice on the part of Louis XV. The restoration of conquests on either side on the continent of Europe, the restoration of Cape Breton Island, the key to French Canada, and, if the demolition of the walls of Dunkirk was demanded, the cession of the fortress of Furnes, were all which the victors of Raucoux and Laufeldt thought it necessary to demand. Terms such as these might well be discussed between the two commanding generals, Marshal Saxe and the Duke of Cumberland. But though the duke and his father would have been glad enough that an opportunity should have been thus

afforded of regaining in diplomacy some of the prestige
that had been lost in war, the English ministry did not
see their way to placing so important a matter in hands
so untried. To Lord Sandwich, who had already acted
as their representative in the futile negotiations of Breda,
was given the real management of the negotiations.

The exclusion of her ambassador from the conferences of 1746 had shown Maria Theresa the course
which was likely to be pursued. Unwilling again to be
left out in the cold, she at once instructed her general,
Bathyany, as to the line he was to pursue, and attempted
to secure his co-operation with the other military
diplomatists. But the appointment of Lord Sandwich
had, in fact, already destroyed the extreme simplicity
aimed at by the French. When the negotiations
passed into diplomatic hands, the claims of the
empress could not be entirely ignored. An interview
between the French foreign minister Puysieux and
Sandwich at Liège resulted in the determination to
hold a general congress, and the appointment of Aix-
la-Chapelle as the place of meeting. The duty of
upholding the claims of Austria was laid upon Kaunitz.
He would willingly now, as at Breda, have avoided the
responsibility. His health was much shaken, and,
unable to see his way to bring the objects he himself
had in view to a successful issue, he would gladly have
declined the post. But the trust of his mistress in his
abilities was too strong to allow her to dispense with
his services. Technical difficulties as to the title under
which he should be received at the congress delayed
for three months his arrival at Aix-la-Chapelle. They
were months of busy intrigue. All the Powers seemed

to have believed that more advantage was to be gained
by private negotiations and separate treaties than by
the general settlement which would be the issue
of the congress, and were each desirous of entering
upon the general discussion with certain points already
secured.   Thus England, taking advantage of the
presence of the Spanish minister Wall, who was
then in London, carried on a close negotiation with
Spain.   The result was not a treaty, but the determination of the English to demand at all hazards
Parma and Piacenza for Don Philip; for so only did it
appear likely that their retention of Gibraltar would be
unquestioned.   Thus again Maria Theresa went even
further in negotiation with France; and, believing that
satisfactory terms had been arrived at, authorised her
ambassador to conclude a preliminary convention.   The
terms of the treaty on which the contracting parties
desired to insist were, generally, the *status quo* before
the war.   In Italy the surrender of Parma and Piacenza
was to be limited by the reservation of the reversion to
Austria and by the countercession of the Stato dei
Presidie to the Duke of Tuscany.   While, most
important of all, any mention of a guarantee to the
King of Prussia for his late acquisition was to be
carefully avoided.   The plenipotentiaries of the two
Powers were to act in unison at the congress for the
purpose of obtaining adherence to these preliminaries.
If they failed to do so, the courts were still to hold
themselves pledged on the matter.   So complete was
the arrangement, that Kaunitz considered it certain
that he could secure these terms, and declared the
completion of this preliminary treaty a master-stroke.

It will be seen at once that as far as Austria was
concerned, the real points at issue were two: her
position in the Italian peninsula, and her position with
regard to Prussia. Smarting bitterly under the loss
of Silesia, Maria Theresa could not bear the idea of
parting with any more of her ancestral dominions.
But by the Treaty of Worms, and for the purpose of
securing the important co-operation of the Sardinian
king, certain districts in the neighbourhood of his
kingdom had been surrendered to him. All her efforts
were therefore directed to avoid the necessity of completing this cession, or of finding by any further
diminution of her dominions the establishment for Don
Philip which the Spaniards persistently claimed. If
either or both of these were demanded from her, some
compensation, she held, was certainly due to her. On
the other hand, she never lost sight of the possibility
of the reopening of the Silesian question, although
content at present to remain true to her promises
contracted at Dresden. In the preliminaries of which
Kaunitz so highly approved, the very probable reversion
of Don Philip's establishment remained to her, the
Presidie recompensed her for the loss of the cessions
of Worms, the refusal of the guarantee of Silesia left
open to her the possibility of regaining it. These were
better terms than she could possibly expect from
England; for the English ministry had given her
clearly to understand that they would require not only
the completion of the Treaty of Worms in favour of the
Sardinian king, but also the cession of Parma and Piacenza
to Don Philip, with the reversion not to Austria but to
the present possessor, who was in fact the Sardinian king.

The attempts of Robinson at Berlin to justify the conduct of his court encountered the bitter anger and scorn of the queen. " Why," she asked, " was she always to be shut out of negotiations which had reference chiefly to her business ?" Thrice already the pressure of the English had driven her to part with portions of her territory. Was she to yield a fourth time ? " Put me in Italy in the same position as I was before the war, and I will make arrangements for the Infanta. But there is your King of Sardinia, who must have everything without the slightest reference to me. Heavens! how am I misused by your Government! Then there is your King of Prussia too. In very truth, all these things taken together rend open too many former wounds, and inflict at the same time new and deadly blows." It was plain that she hoped more from her enemies than from her friends. Both she and Kaunitz recognised that the key of the difficulty lay with France, and, apparently forgetting that they had absolutely nothing to offer which could induce it to make a separate treaty, deceived themselves with the belief that France would prefer friendship with Austria to peace with England. Nor was their belief unreasonable, considering the state which the negotiations they had carried on had now reached. As Kaunitz said, he had indeed no reason to believe that the assertions of the French ambassador were untrue. Great therefore was the shock when on the evening of April 30, at a dinner he had himself given to the ambassadors, he was told by Lord Sandwich that the preliminaries had been already settled between the French and the Maritime Powers. The party which had most to offer had naturally been the favoured one in the bargain.

The terms of the preliminary treaty, when known, were no surprise to Kaunitz or to Maria Theresa. They were in fact those which had been always explained to her by Robinson at Vienna. All conquests both in Europe and in the Colonies were to be returned. Dunkirk maintained its fortifications upon the land side, but was stripped of them towards the sea. Parma, Piacenza, and Guastalla were given to Don Philip, with reversion to the present owner. Modena and Genoa kept what they held before the war. The cessions of the Worms Treaty, with the exception of Piacenza, were confirmed to Charles Emanuel. England obtained a renewal of the Assiento, and a guarantee for the Hanoverian succession. Francis was recognised as emperor; and the Pragmatic Sanction, modified only by what was given to Prussia and Sardinia, was guaranteed. Frederick was secured in the possession of Silesia and Glatz. A secret clause declared that any Power which should refuse to accept these conditions would lose the advantages of the treaty. But if the Austrian court and its representative had no reason to be surprised at the terms which had been agreed to, they had much room for displeasure, and Kaunitz was not slow in showing it in very outspoken language addressed to the French plenipotentiary. Yet he could not but confess that the strength of the English position had been overwhelming, and he appears immediately to have suppressed his anger against the French, and to have turned it in full stream upon his late allies. It was to them alone that he could attribute terms so distasteful to his mistress.

From Vienna instructions reached him to declare that as far as the objects of the war were concerned the empress would at once accept them, but that she could not conceive that the relations between herself and her allies had anything whatever to do with the conclusion of peace ; while as to the Prussian guarantee, she could only conceive that it was intended, not as a one-sided support of Prussian encroachments, but as a general guarantee of the Dresden Treaty. In that sense she was ready to accept it.

The preliminaries were not so well received by the parties concerned as to destroy all hope that they might be changed in the definitive treaty ; and suggestions of different combinations were freely handed to and fro, always to encounter a fatal opposition from some one of the interested courts, and always rendered nugatory by the same flaw in the position of Austria,—the absence of any advantage to offer to France. It is in fact difficult to believe that the French diplomatists were serious in their suggestions, or had any other object in view than that which St. Severin clearly expresses when he writes to the foreign minister, " that the great advantage of the whole course of negotiation lay in the fact that, for years to come, Austria and Sardinia would not forget the trick which the Maritime Powers had played them." It was not with England alone that difficulties arose. The method in which the restitution of the Low Countries, contemplated in the preliminaries, was to be effected produced a sharp quarrel with Holland. While the empress demanded that both country and fortresses should be handed directly back to her, and pointed out the absurdity of the Dutch claim to garrison cities which they had been so unable to hold, and which the French had since razed to the ground, the Dutch asserted the lasting validity of the Barrier Treaty, and the evident intention of the empress to free herself from its restrictions.

The futility of the struggle for improved terms gradually forced itself upon the mind of the empress. She became more eager than her ministers for the conclusion of peace. On some points she would not absolutely yield. At all events she determined to show the world that the treaty was contracted without her co-operation and against her will. For the sake of peace she was ready to allow Kaunitz to append his signature, but instructed him that unless important alterations were made in several of the articles, and in particular with respect to the Barrier fortresses, he must withhold that signature for some little time. The alterations were not made. On October 18 the treaty was signed by the representatives of England, Holland, and France, and by degrees the other Powers accepted it also. The last to hold out was the King of Sardinia, whose representative did not sign till November 17.

The impression made upon the mind both of Maria Theresa and of her minister Kaunitz by the lengthened transactions which were concluded at Aix-la-Chapelle was of the widest significance. The course of the war had already taught many of the wiser heads in Vienna that the real danger to Austria lay, not in France, but in Prussia. It did not require much observation to see that for the purpose of opposing the new enemy, the old alliance with the Maritime Powers had lost much of its value. As long as the traditional enmity with France had existed, nothing could have been more advantageous. The Low Countries were the natural battleground between France and England ; and though they were indeed an Austrian possession, their distance from the centre of the Empire preserved the German States from danger, while the struggle upon the sea constantly ate into the resources of France. But now a Power unsurpassed, it was believed, in its military resources became a far more desirable ally in a war which was to be waged on land and in the heart of Germany. Circumstances had made it plain that there was no absolute impossibility in winning the friendship of that Power, hostile though it had always hitherto been. At the same time England had been found an inconvenient ally, setting high value upon the money assistance it contributed, and in its single-minded and obstinate determination to direct the war against France alone, always inclined to demand sacrifices for the general good, with very little respect to the individual interests of its allies.

CHAPTER IV

MARIA THERESA'S EARLY REFORMS

1748-1757

"WHAT troubles me most is the impatience of the empress to see the return of her troops, lest delay should upset the system of Haugwitz. The fear of this plunges her from time to time into terrible outbursts of impatience, and gives birth to all sorts of strange ideas, such as giving *carte blanche* to the English to negotiate for us, in the hope of thus hastening the conclusion of peace and the return of the troops." So writes the Chancellor Ulfeld to Kaunitz, the negotiator at Aix-la-Chapelle, in July 1748. In fact Maria Theresa had for some time been eager for peace, and willing to pay the required price for it. The eight years' war had given lessons which her sagacious mind was fully able to appreciate. It is true that she had emerged from the lengthened struggle with an amount of success which her most sanguine friends could scarcely have hoped for at the beginning of her reign. She still maintained her foremost place among the princes of Europe. None the less a rich province

had been torn from her dominion ; her arms had been
constantly worsted by a new and upstart Power; and
she had more than once found herself compelled to pursue
a line of conduct thoroughly repugnant to her own will.

It was no doubt by her allies rather than by her
enemies that these humiliations had been forced upon
her.   But that allies so little to her taste should have
been indispensable was in itself a proof of her weakness ;
and the cause of that weakness she had learned to find
chiefly in the errors of the system of government with
which she was inevitably entangled.   It was impossible
that a young woman, whose education in the art of
government had been recklessly disregarded, while
every step was being taken to secure her unbroken
succession to vast and inharmonious dominions, should
be able at once to free herself either from the policy or
from the advisers she had inherited.   It was out of the
question that even if she had a clear will of her own,
she should have had confidence enough to assert it.
The ruins left by the decay of the system of the Middle
Ages encumbered on all sides the march of government.
The policy followed for many years by the Austrian
House was too deeply imprinted on the minds of her
aged councillors to allow of any adaptation to the
changed circumstances of Europe; while the rivalry
and self-seeking of her ministers prevented them from
giving any advice of a large or general character.   As
she herself said, when reviewing the earlier events of
her reign, in words which applied to more than one
generation of ministers, she found herself "without an
army, without money, without credit, without experience or knowledge of her own, and even without

F

counsel, because every minister gave his first attention to observe how the matter in consideration would affect himself." The first eight years of her reign had thoroughly changed her position. "Providence," as she expressed it, "had relieved her by death of councillors too prejudiced to give useful advice, but too respectable and meritorious to be dismissed." Experience had taught her her own value; she felt herself freed from the necessity of leaning upon the advice even of her husband. Full of the conscientious intention, which from the first moment of her reign she had formed— to rule strictly for the good of her people; humiliated by the sense of powerlessness which had been forced upon her by the events of the late war; determined some time or other to recover her lost provinces, or some equivalent for them; and regarding the Peace of Aix-la-Chapelle as merely a temporary arrangement (so certain was she of the aggressive tendencies of the Prussian king), she longed eagerly for a quiet period, which might afford her an opportunity of giving effect to the great reforms she had meditated.

For she had taken stock of her position, and had gauged the weakness of the prevalent system of government. At the root of the evil lay the broken and disjointed character of the Austrian monarchy. This inheritance from the Feudal System made itself visible in every branch of the government. It was not only that the kingdom itself consisted of various provinces ruled by different titles, and under different constitutions; provincialism and aristocratic independence permeated the whole body-politic. The cure, she believed, lay in the realisation of what was already becoming the political ideal of the time,—the establishment of a benevolent despotism, the increase of the powers of the central state, and the supremacy of the sovereign over the local noble. At the same time she saw clearly that the conditions of Europe had entirely changed. The chief duty of Austria in the European system was no longer to serve as a balance to the power of the Bourbons; self-preservation from the threatened encroachments of a restless neighbour had become a far more crying necessity. The system of treaties and alliances required by the one object might not be suitable to the other; and though as yet she had no immediate intention of adopting a remodelled policy, she already saw that sooner or later such a step might be necessary. To give a practical effect to this conception of a new and changed world, like-minded ministers were a matter of necessity. Such ministers were found in three men who, though they did not stand alone, may be regarded as the chief agents in the great work of creating modern Austria. They were Ludwig Haugwitz and Rudolf Chotek, and, in a still greater degree, Wenzel Count Kaunitz. Though the peculiar work of Kaunitz was the management of foreign affairs, and though his chief activity belongs to a somewhat later period, his great ability was already appreciated by Maria Theresa, and a close personal friendship arose between them, which gave him a predominant influence in all branches of the government. He was consulted in every difficulty, and his opinion was sought upon every question which arose.

After so many years of war, it was natural that the attention of Maria Theresa should be first directed to

the need of reform in the army. Its comparative
weakness and the want of means for its efficient
maintenance had been the cause of her losses, and of
the humiliation she had suffered at the hand of her
allies. The need of centralisation was sufficiently
obvious. The troops of each province were raised
only when required, and were maintained by the
provincial Estates; a yearly grant settled both the
number of men and the amount of money that were
needed; and the troops were supplied with most of
the necessaries of life (quartering, food, forage, horses,
etc.) by taxes in kind. The inevitable consequence of
this arrangement was that the Estates of each province
confined themselves as closely as possible to their own
actual needs, and, neglecting the general welfare of the
Empire, attempted to throw the lion's share of the
public burdens on the other provinces. It was to this
that might be traced the paucity of troops in Silesia
and Bohemia which had given Frederick his opportunity.
To Maria Theresa, threatened, as she believed herself to
be, on all sides, it seemed impossible that such an
arrangement could afford proper protection to her
dominions; while she could not but regard as somewhat derogatory to her position the necessity of de-
manding year by year from the Estates supplies so
grudgingly granted.

    In Count Haugwitz she found an efficient instrument
for carrying out the changes she regarded as necessary.
A Silesian nobleman of high standing, he had won her
confidence by his firm adhesion to the interests of
Austria and by his well-known mistrust of the Prussian
king. His views, which were reported to her by her

secretary, Koch, were exactly in harmony with her own. The safety of the Empire, he said, depended on the establishment of the immediate supremacy of the sovereign over the army, and the maintenance of an adequate body of troops even in time of peace. The mind of Maria Theresa was always singularly open to advice. It seems to have been her habit to listen to the suggestions even of a private person, and, if they appeared to be fruitful, to demand from their author a full exposition of his views. In accordance with this practice, Haugwitz was requested to formulate his ideas. He at once produced a plan for giving them practical effect. In his opinion, the security of the Empire required an army of at least 108,000 men, and for their maintenance an annual sum of 14,000,000 gulden, an increase of not less than five million on the ordinary contribution from the Estates. To avoid obstruction or fluctuations in the amount of the grant, he recommended that it should be settled for a period of ten years. As all would profit by the security thus obtained, all, whether noble or peasant, should pay their share of the required contribution. A compensation for the increase of the taxes might be found in the abolition of all payments in kind. The empress would thus find herself in possession of an army sufficiently strong for the purposes of the Empire, a certain income on which to support it, and free from all the trammels which the interference of the aristocratic Estates had hitherto laid upon her. The army would thus assume the character of a national army, and could be reorganised in the complete form which Frederick had taught the world to be necessary for success. These were great and

obvious advantages, but the real importance of the
scheme was political, and consisted in the establishment
of the unchecked supremacy of the State. Not only
was the army withdrawn from interference on the part
of the Estates, but the most dearly-cherished privileges
of the nobles were directly assaulted. Their freedom
from taxation, which proved elsewhere, and especially
in France, the great stumbling-block to improved administration, was to be taken from them. No sort of
property was to be exempted from the incidence of the
tax; property and rent were alike subjected to it. Full
equality was not indeed arrived at; the rent-payer was
still rated more highly than the proprietor; but the
great principle of universal liability to the bearing of
the public burdens was laid down.

So grave an assault upon their privileges could not
pass without resistance from the privileged classes. The
leadership of the opposition, when the plan was brought
before the Conference, was assumed by Count Frederick
Harrach, whose family connections and high official
standing placed him at the head of the greater nobility.
He was not only a member of the Conference and High
Chancellor of Bohemia, but as representative of his
brother Ferdinand (who was absent in Lombardy), he was
Land Marshal of the archduchy of Austria beyond the
Enns. So formidable an opponent was not to be easily
worsted, nor was a man whose ability had marked him
out as the fitting negotiator of the Treaty of Dresden
likely to fail in resource. He at once produced a plan of
reform, of an exactly contrary character to that supplied
by Haugwitz; all the requirements of the Exchequer
were to be covered by an annual grant *en bloc* from the

Estates. Much as the other members of the Conference sympathised with Harrach, they regarded with dismay so vast and sudden an extension of the power of the Estates, and Maria Theresa found it possible to induce them to give their approval to the scheme of Haugwitz, which is known as the Ten Years' Recess. The battle was thus half won, but there still remained the opposition of the Estates themselves to be overcome. It was only after the lapse of several years, and by the exertion (in the case of Carinthia at least) of despotic authority, that the measure was accepted in the German and Bohemian provinces.

The reorganisation of the army was the immediate result of the adoption of the Ten Years' Recess. Considering the large measure of success which had attended its efforts, the irregularity and shapelessness of the Austrian army as an instrument of warfare are almost incredible. It was now gradually brought into order. Uniformity of dress and of arms was introduced. Some similarity in the numbers constituting a regiment, the reduction of the irregular troops to discipline, the formation of the soldiers of the frontier into regiments, the strict repression of military excesses, some attempt to imitate the rapid firing and manœuvring of the Prussian troops, in fact all those details of organisation which constitute the idea of a modern army, were the fruit of the concentration of the Austrian forces in the hands of the crown. To bring them to the test of practical experience, camps of exercise and military manœuvres were organised, and were often visited by the empress herself, who also showed how clearly she understood one of the chief necessities of a good army by establishing institutions for the scientific education of her officers. Something approaching to general conscription was adopted, and a very efficient instrument was called into existence. Its efficiency was still, however, somewhat limited by the restriction of the officers' commissions to men of noble birth.

The reformation of the army was but a preliminary step. The empress, still acting under the advice of Haugwitz, pushed the same principles into the reform of every branch of the government. The double chancery of Bohemia and of Austria, which had hitherto rendered all unity of government impossible, was fused in the single Directorium. Subordinate courts, known as Representations, responsible only to the Directorium, and exercising their functions locally, were established in the various provinces; and the constant presence of the central power was made still more obvious by the establishment of District Councils (Kreis-ämter). No institution probably exerted a more lasting influence upon Austrian life than this. These District Councils, which were royal courts, were charged with the duty of bringing to the notice of the Representations all abuses, and all evasions of commands emanating from the crown. They thus gradually acquired authority in every branch of government. They even superseded the communal arrangements of the cities, took the police into their hands, and acquired the management of the communal property. But more than all else, they became the guardians of the rights of the peasantry against the encroachments of their lords, and against the evils which the perpetuation of the remnants of the Feudal System inevitably caused.

The centralisation of administration went hand in hand with the division of the functions of government. Justice, which had been supervised by the old Chanceries, was now separated from the Directorium. A High Court of Justice was established, with paramount authority over the whole system of judicature. Such a centralisation, by bringing to light the great variety of usage in different forms of court and in different provinces, led the way to an attempt to codify the existing laws. The wide difference between the constituent provinces of the Austrian dominions at once became evident. Several commissions sitting in the capitals of the various provinces were constituted, and the commissioners soon found that in order to give the work its proper success, not a mere codification, but an entire remodelling and unification of the civil law was necessary. In February 1753 a commission was appointed to prepare a new code of civil procedure for all the German provinces. But though many years of able and intelligent labour were devoted to this great work, the difficulties and opposition it encountered were so great that when it was produced in 1766 it was found necessary still further to postpone its practical employment. A similar code for the criminal law met with somewhat better success, and was adopted in 1768.

No doubt the measures which were taken for centralising the administration were imperfect, unprogressive, and containing the seeds of evil. Read in the light of present history, the nullification of the powers of the Estates, instead of the broadening of the basis on which the Estates rested, has a reactionary appearance. The highly-centralised state system thus introduced led

directly to a lifeless bureaucracy. But the prescience
even of the greatest statesman is never very far-reaching,
and must necessarily be limited by the knowledge and
temper of the time. It was no slight exhibition of
statesmanlike ability to carry through reforms which
remodelled every branch of government, and, by infusing
new vigour into every department, to save an empire
which seemed rapidly falling into complete dilapidation.
Popular forces played as yet no part in the reckoning of
statesmen. It was much that a sovereign power should
consciously assume the position of guardian of the well-
being of every class of subject, and become the fertile,
if arbitrary, source of reform.

The same spirit of arbitrary and paternal reform
inspired the changes in domestic legislation carried out
by the empress with the assistance of Rudolf Chotek.
The rival, nay, enemy of Haugwitz, he yet worked in
the same direction. He found his special sphere of
activity in the management of the indirect taxes, the
taxes upon consumption and kindred subjects. Chotek
was no freer than Haugwitz from the limitations of the
time; the mercantile system still bore unbroken sway
in the realm of political economy. But he had the
merit of clearly recognising that the strength of a
country lay chiefly in the wellbeing of the people, and
devoted himself zealously to promote it by measures
which tended always to the unification of the Empire
and the supremacy of the State. Economically, his
measures were strictly in accordance with the old
theory; high, sometimes prohibitive, tariffs guarded
the frontier and protected the producer; privileges and
monopolies were used to excite industry; royal establish-

ments, loans, and premiums created fresh forms of manufacture irrespective of the natural demand. But the great evil of Austria, the separation of its many provinces, was somewhat remedied by the diminution of internal tolls, while intercourse was rendered easy by the development of a fine system of roads. This great advantage was secured by a tax in which no exemption of the nobles was allowed.

The avowed object of the protective system was to increase the power of the people to meet a higher taxation. It was supposed that the tax-payer receiving higher prices for his goods could pay more to the State. As in the case of the direct contribution, the burdens of the people were not lessened, but, on the contrary, were considerably increased during this period of peace. Haugwitz had earned general hatred for himself and his Silesian colleagues, but it was small when compared with the hatred which fell upon Chotek. Nor did the system work always in favour even of the unity of the Empire. Hungary was, as a matter of course, excluded from the reforms in the tolls and tariffs. Markets for the rich produce of this country might naturally have been found in the Austrian provinces; but on the supposition that unless prices were maintained the taxes could not be paid, the high tariffs to the disadvantage of Hungary were kept up. The corn-growers and cattle-dealers of the valleys of the Danube and the Theiss were taught to seek their customers in foreign lands. That the divisions of the Empire were thus widened is evident; yet even this mistaken policy produced certain advantages. An exit for Hungarian goods was necessary, and Trieste and Fiume became important commercial centres of sufficient activity to excite the envy of the Venetian traders.

The benevolent despotism, which was the characteristic of the renovated Austria, did not confine itself to the physical wellbeing of the people. Intelligent obedience in the subject, well-ordered industry in the producer, education and training in the governing classes were necessary conditions of success in the development of the new system, and were inconsistent with the prevalent laxity of morals, rough manners, gross ignorance, and superstition. The improvement of education, emanating, like the rest of the system, from a central authority, received therefore much attention. Though the primary schools were not thoroughly reorganised till somewhat later, steps in the right direction were already taken; such as the regulation of the schools in Tyrol in 1747, and the general order that schoolmasters were to be chosen from experienced and respectable men. A well-arranged and stringent system of examinations breathed new life into the secondary schools or gymnasiums; and a plan was set on foot for establishing a whole system of technical education, with the object of improving, by theoretical knowledge, the practical work of the manufacturing classes. The curriculum was scarcely different from that of similar institutions at the present time. Not only was the conception of the instruction of the working classes unusually enlightened, the admission of laymen to the position of instructors shows an unexpected advance in liberal thought, at a time when all education in Austria was in the hands either of the Jesuits or of the order of the Piarists.

In the higher walks of education, in the University, a thorough reform was instituted. Higher rank and higher salaries were attached to the professoriate, with the object of attracting able men from other countries. New and better methods of instruction were devised and insisted upon. The University jurisdiction was strictly limited. A head of each faculty was appointed, under whom the professors worked; while over the whole was placed the Archbishop von Trautzen, as director of studies, armed with very arbitrary powers. Finally, by the absorption of the property of the University, and by the payment of all the teachers by Government, the University ceased to be an independent corporation, and became a department of the State. There is no doubt that from this reform, as from all the others, great improvement at once resulted; though it restricted independence both of thought and action, and rendered possible the evils of over-regulation and of bureaucratic rule.

The name of Van Swieten, the empress's confidential physician and friend, to whose inspiration the educational enthusiasm of the reign is chiefly due, worthily takes its place by the side of those of the three statesmen already mentioned as the main agents in the renovation of Austria.

These wide-spreading reforms, falling little short of the reconstitution of the country upon a new and more modern basis, were confined to the central provinces of the Austrian empire. There are abundant indications that Maria Theresa would gladly have extended them to her three great outlying territories, Hungary, Lombardy, and the Netherlands. But her ready recognition of the limits of her power, and her fine sense of the restrictions laid upon it by circumstance, which place her states-manship in so strong a contrast with the unmodified legislation of her son, induced her early to withdraw from any attempt to complete her scheme of centralisa-tion in the face of strong opposition.

Her position in these three territories was very different. In Hungary, where she occupied a throne long in the possession of her family, she found herself at the head of a free people, or rather a predominant aristocracy, who regarded with intense jealousy any infringement of their privileges, any step which threatened to assimilate their country to the other less-favoured portions of their sovereign's dominions. Lombardy, an acquisition of only some forty years ago, had scarcely reconciled itself to its change of masters, and was far more closely connected, both by manners and by family ties, with the Spaniards, from whom it had been taken. In the Netherlands, the existence of the Barrier Treaty seemed even to call in question the full sovereignty of the empress, and to render her position and conduct there a matter of international policy.

There was no doubt a strong temptation long felt by the Austrian court to bring the jealous and privileged country of Hungary (which lay so close to the centre of the Empire, and which, as late events had shown, was so important a factor in its power) into closer relation with the other provinces, and to obliterate the distinctions which had so often rendered it a source of danger rather than of strength. It was impossible for a sovereign with a keen sense of justice and a strong desire for the unity of her dominions,—feelings which had indeed been the

cause of the late war,—to see burdens laid with an un-
sparing hand on one part of her empire, while a second
part, as well able to bear them, was allowed to remain
comparatively free.   When rearranging her revenue
and providing means for the maintenance of the army,
Maria Theresa had been struck by the fact that the
contribution of Hungary amounted to little more than a
third of that paid by Bohemia, although in territory,
wealth and population it was the richer country of the
two.   Though the support afforded her at the beginning
of her reign, and the enthusiasm with which it was
granted, have been much exaggerated, there is no doubt
that assistance of a very substantial nature had been
given her by Hungary.   She was not ungrateful for it.
She had attached to herself and her court, in a way unknown to her predecessors, many of the great Hungarian
nobles ; and now, trusting to their support, in spite of
warnings given her by some of them, she determined to
attempt the removal of the injustice which had struck
her.   She even hoped that the friendly relations she had
established would enable her to carry her propositions
with such general approval that the world would see
"that Hungary, of old the constant seat of intrigue
against the Austrian House, had laid aside its jealousy,
and was ready to join willingly in the defence of the
Empire."   The Diet of 1751 showed her the vanity of
this hope.   Though she gave up all idea of bringing the
nobles within the limits of taxation, though she demanded
only the very moderate increase of 120,000 gulden to
the contribution, and though she enjoyed the full support
of the Upper House of Magnates, her proposal met with
a storm of opposition.   The contest raged for many

weeks. It assumed the constitutional form so well
known in parliamentary history, the refusal on the one
side to grant supplies till grievances were removed, and
on the other to accept the required grant upon conditions.
Eventually, though with a bad grace, a sort of compromise was arrived at. The empress accepted about
half the sum she had demanded, the Diet had to rest
contented with a vague promise that their grievances
should be attended to. Any attempt to limit the power
of the nobles, or to introduce a well-ordered administration having its source in the sovereign, was laid aside.

With regard to the two other territories, the empress
desired to establish in them subordinate branches of her
House. As long as the war lasted, the position of the
Austrians in Milan was difficult. Close connections
existed between the Lombard nobility and the Spaniards,
and the people felt more sympathy with the cognate
race, who had so long ruled them, than for their new
Teutonic governors. Intrigues and, from the German
point of view, treasonable correspondences were of
constant occurrence. But, on the whole, Maria Theresa
appears to have understood the difficulties of her
subjects, and, with a few exceptions, pardons for
treasonable conduct were easily procured upon renewed
declarations of loyalty. This gentle handling produced
good results. After the Peace of Aix-la-Chapelle, and
the Conference of Nice, where in the following year
many of the smaller difficulties of the peninsula were
cleared up, little more is heard of treason. The management of Lombardy was in the hands of a council in
Vienna, and, subject to its supervision, of a viceroy
appointed for three years and living in Milan. Count

Ferdinand Harrach and Count Lucas John Pallavicini in
turn occupied this position. Harrach was well fitted for
the conciliatory part he had to play, and succeeded in
winning the goodwill of the Italians, and thus preparing
the way for the exaction of a larger revenue, the one
permanent object of the Austrian court. An increased
army, with money to maintain it, was the first point at
which Maria Theresa aimed. To wring an increase of
payment from the provinces of Northern Italy was a
difficult task, but Pallavicini and his more able assistant,
the Grand Chancellor Christiani, found means to solve
it. A new survey of property and settlement of a land
tax, a well-judged arrangement for the farming of the
indirect taxes, and a consolidation of the public debt
produced the required increase without hampering the
industry of the people. The new view of the supremacy
of the State was shown in the withdrawal from the
Church of its immunity from taxation. The measure
was not completed till after negotiation with Pope
Benedict XIV. in 1757, and was only partial ; yet, by
establishing the principle that church property was
liable to taxation, it was a distinct advance in the
direction of removal of privilege. With these exceptions, there is no sign of attempt at centralisation.
In the hands of Christiani, a man who had forced his
way to the front in spite of unattractive exterior and
uncourtly manners, and had won the confidence not only
of his own court but of the Italian Powers by whom he
was surrounded, the action of the Government was
wholly beneficial. It seemed indeed to tend rather in
the direction of self-government than in that of bureaucracy. The Communes were allowed on many points

G

to rule themselves, all tax-payers were members of the general Communal Assembly, three elected officers formed a permanent executive committee. This freedom, coupled with the settlement of the land tax, did much for the encouragement of agriculture, and left a lasting impression upon the Lombard people.

Christiani crowned his success by suggesting, and carrying out, an arrangement exactly in harmony with the wishes of the empress, and aided by her strenuous support. It was directed to the establishment of one of the princes of the Austrian House in a very commanding and independent position. To secure this end, he took advantage of the condition of the reigning family of Modena, and the character of its head. Attached to the French interest during the War of Succession, Francis III. of Modena had been reinstated at the peace. His son, Prince Hercules, had married the wealthy heiress of Massa and Carrara. One daughter was the offspring of this marriage, and, as her parents had quarrelled and separated, she was heiress of the whole property of her mother and grandfather. Christiani sought to secure this rich princess for one of the Austrian archdukes, and with her the succession to her great inheritance. The showy and extravagant character of Francis III. gave him his opportunity, and enabled him to contract a treaty by which the young princess became the betrothed wife of the Archduke Leopold, or, failing him, one of his younger brothers, on whom Modena was to be settled. In exchange for this concession, Francis was to be made viceroy at Milan, and supplied with large revenues and every opportunity for self-indulgence, till the young archduke was fitted to take his place. As no good

government could be expected from Francis, Christiani
himself was placed at his side as minister plenipotentiary.
If this scheme succeeded, an Austrian archduke would
sooner or later occupy the throne of the united countries
of Lombardy and Modena.

The same idea of establishing, in her more distant
dominions, princes of her own House in a position of
much independence, appears again in the conduct Maria
Theresa pursued in the Low Countries. She had married
her sister Marianne to her husband's brother, Prince
Charles of Lorraine, and had placed the Low Countries
under their government. As she herself says, when
writing immediately after the death of her sister in
1745 : "In the midst of the misfortunes of my reign, I
had no other consolation than the establishment of the
two Houses [that is, her own and her sister's], which
would afford each other mutual support, not so much for
the aggrandisement of my successors, as for the advantage
of the countries over which they ruled." This hope had
disappeared at the premature death of the princess ; and
the years following, until the Treaty of Aix-la-Chapelle
was signed, had been a period of bitter suffering and
disaster. For the Low Countries had been the constant
scene of warfare, and a prey to the armies of France,
whose moderation under such circumstances was not
notorious. Kaunitz, who as minister plenipotentiary
carried on the government in the Netherlands, had been
a sympathetic but powerless witness of the suffering.

The return of peace enabled Charles of Lorraine to
resume his office, having as his chief adviser the Marquis
Botta d'Adorno. It is strange to see a man, whose
mismanagement had allowed the Austrians to be driven

so ignominiously from Genoa, raised to so important a position. But his abilities as a financier led to his appointment, and his success fully justified it. The period of the viceroyalty of Charles and the ministry of Botta is one of the most calm and prosperous in Belgian history. Their work was chiefly directed to alleviate the misery caused by the war and to establish commercial prosperity. Although the constitution was exactly of the sort most opposed to the new principles adopted by Maria Theresa, allowing, as it did, large rights of self-government and many privileges to the noble and clerical estates, no attempt was made to change it. For there was a very wholesome dread of the opposition which might be aroused if innovations were introduced. The conduct of Maria Theresa and her ministers in the Netherlands was therefore conciliatory and prudent. Their introduction of reforms was gradual and un-ostentatious. The co-operation of the people themselves was sought ; and no effort was spared to persuade them that the intentions of the Government were entirely benevolent. It was thus with mixed motives that Maria Theresa involved herself in opposition to the Barrier Treaty. There was no doubt a real recognition of the injury it inflicted upon her subjects. But the warmth with which she took up the quarrel must be partly attributed to the more refined political object of winning the confidence of the people before entering upon reforms which should bring the constitution of the Netherlands into harmony with her general principles of government.

CHAPTER V

THE administrative reforms, connected chiefly with the name of Haugwitz, were for the most part highly beneficial. In many respects they were conceived in a spirit of broad liberality not often seen in the history of Austria. But in appreciating the character of the empress, too much stress must not be laid either upon the liberality or the beneficence. It is true that she had adopted a noble conception of the duties of a sovereign, and that she was gifted with a sensibility easily touched by the joys and sorrows of her people. But the overmastering inspiration of her actions lay not so much in her desire to secure their happiness as in her determination to support the greatness of the state, the efficiency of the army, and the acquisition of an adequate and permanent revenue. To these objects were subordinated all administrative and financial measures. Even her care for education was practical rather than theoretical; it was not her love of learning, but the desire to create good servants of the state,

which actuated her. Her reforms, however, had
launched her on a course of innovation; and circumstances were rapidly leading her to recognise that an
even more complete breach with the traditions of the
past might be advantageous in the external relations
of the empire. Already more than once during the
continuance of the war, critical moments had occurred,
when the possibility and advantage of an entire change
of front had flashed across her. After the conclusion of
peace, and the hard struggle which had attended the
negotiations at Aix-la-Chapelle, the idea was so prominent in her mind that she determined to consider
it formally, and requested each of the ministers of
the Conference to put into writing their view of the
political system, and the line of conduct in respect to
European friendships and alliances which they thought
it most advisable for Austria to pursue. She even
induced her husband to join in this important and
formal discussion. With more or less variation in
their arguments, all the members of the Conference
agreed with the emperor that, in spite of the slights
which Austria had received from England, the true
policy to pursue consisted in the maintenance of close
friendly relations with the Maritime Powers, and with
Russia, so far as consistent policy was possible in dealing
with a country so dependent upon the personal character
and whims of its rulers.

To the general acceptance of this view there was,
however, one exception, and that a most important one.
The youngest member of the Conference was Wenzel,
Count Kaunitz. The second son of Count Max Ulrich
Kaunitz and Countess Marie Rietberg, his full title was

Count Kaunitz Rietberg. Both his parents were
members of the higher nobility. His father appears
to have been a man of considerable influence, and his
mother was undoubtedly a woman of unusually strong,
almost masculine character, who impressed her in-
dividuality forcibly upon her daughters, to whose
education she was devoted. How far she participated
in the training of her son's mind is uncertain. After
the usual fashion of the younger sons of noble houses,
he was intended for the Church, and in accordance
with the abuse of Church preferment prevalent at that
time in Europe, and especially in Austria, before he was
thirteen years of age he was endowed with a canonry.
But the death of his elder brother changed his career.
His talents were henceforward devoted to the service
of the state ; and with this object in view he studied
law and cognate subjects in Vienna, Leipzig, and
Leyden. After putting a finishing touch to his education by a lengthened tour, during which he visited
Italy, France, and England, he returned to Vienna,
and before the completion of his twenty-fourth year
entered upon public business with the title of *Reichs-
hofrath.* In March 1741 he had been entrusted with
the honourable mission of carrying to the Pope,
Benedict XIV., and to Charles Emanuel the tidings
of the birth of the archduke, who was afterwards
Joseph II. The insight Kaunitz had displayed in his
appreciation of the position of the Italian courts,
pointed him out as a fitting person to carry on the
negotiations at Turin, where the character of the king
and of his minister, the Marquis d'Ormea, seemed to
demand the presence of an ambassador of more than

usual ability. His efforts at completing a treaty were
not successful. The obstinate determination of the
Sardinian court to preserve its independent position
between the great contending Powers, dragged out
the negotiations. Kaunitz returned to Vienna, and
after a brief period of retirement was entrusted with
the management of the Low Countries as minister
plenipotentiary of the nominal but absentee governor.
He had there watched the futile efforts of the allies to
stem the tide of French conquest, and while upholding
the cause of his country in the diplomatic battle of
Aix-la-Chapelle, had been convinced of the advantages
to be derived from a new system of alliances. Admitted
to the Conference on the conclusion of the peace, he had
now an opportunity of elaborating his views.

In his written opinion, with all the fulness and prolixity which marks his State papers, Kaunitz criticised
the political conditions of Europe. He confessed that
England and Holland in connection with Russia and
Saxony were the natural friends of Austria, and that
Turkey, France, and Prussia were its natural enemies.
But from the friends experience had shown that little
assistance was to be expected ; England and Holland
had objects of their own, which were not those of
Austria; no dependence could be placed on Russia ;
and Saxony made no secret of its inability to enter
into war at present. Of the enemies, Turkey might be
regarded as a permanent danger, to be always watched,
but beyond the reach of systematic treatment. The
conduct of France in taking advantage of the weakness
and inexperience of the young empress, the double-
dealing of Fleury, and the success with which a new

opponent to the Austrian House had been established
in Germany, all marked it out as a most dangerous foe.
Yet by far the worst enemy was Frederick of Prussia.
He could not believe that the conquest of Silesia would
be forgotten; his policy would inevitably be directed to
secure his grip on that province. Between him and
Austria a quarrel existed which nothing could appease.
The one absolute necessity in any future system of
external policy was not only watchfulness against the
hostility of Prussia, but its reduction to a condition
which would allow its hostile efforts to be regarded
without fear and the lost provinces to be recovered.
To gain that end alliances were necessary. As no
support in such an object could be expected from
England, where the feeling in favour of Prussia was
strong, there remained but one course, somehow or
other, by means direct or indirect, to secure the
assistance of France. Kaunitz never wavered in his
belief that self-interest alone was the guiding principle
of politics. The advantages which would accrue to
France must, he said, be clearly demonstrated before
its friendship was obtained. He believed that he saw
an opportunity for offering the required advantages, in
an exchange which might be effected between the
Italian duchies, now held by Don Philip, and either
Savoy or the Low Countries. The strong wish of the
French king that his son-in-law's establishment should
be in immediate connection with France would thus be
satisfied. Even if Louis could not be induced to give
overt assistance to an attack upon Prussia, he might give
money, while Spain was put forward as the ostensible
representative of the Bourbon House. The mere fact

that France looked with favour upon the attack would
be enough to produce it. The greedy courts of the
smaller German states would be ready to arm; the
Elector-Palatine and Saxony, backed up by Russia,
would take the opportunity of giving effect to their
jealousy; nay, even Hanover, under such circumstances,
might lend a helping hand.

The arguments of Kaunitz appear to have met with
acceptance, and to have formed a sort of programme
which, sometimes prominently in the front, and sometimes, as circumstances changed, relegated to the background, became henceforward the accepted basis of
Austrian policy. Kaunitz had himself advised that no
time should be lost; for the circumstances of the French
court, the weakness of the French Government, the
suffering and want produced by the late war, and the
mistrust aroused by Frederick's conduct at the Peace
of Dresden, seemed to offer an opportunity which should
not be neglected. But the strong opinion of the emperor,
and even of Maria Theresa, that the maintenance of
old alliances was for the present a matter of necessity,
prevented any immediate or definite action. The whole
diplomatic skill of Austria was, however, henceforward
directed to the quiet undermining of the friendship
between France and Prussia. There can be no doubt
that from this time onwards Maria Theresa and her
ministers were engaged in a secret conspiracy against
Frederick. They did not hide from themselves the
extreme difficulty of the operation. Any premature
disclosure would be fraught with ruin, and might well
leave them still without connection with France, while
deserted by the Maritime Powers. Indeed, in the entire

uncertainty which they felt as to the success of their
manœuvres, it was necessary to continue their existing
system of alliances.   Thus in October 1750 England
was induced to join in the treaty contracted with
Russia in 1746, with the exception always of those
separate articles which were most threatening to
Frederick.   Thus too it was in close connection with
England (and in fact at the suggestion of the English
court) that an effort was made to secure the election
of Maria Theresa's eldest son Joseph as King of the
Romans, and it was the influence of France and Prussia
combined which thwarted the effort.   There was not
the slightest sign as yet of any dissolution of either
partnership, though the same causes which had already
excited Maria Theresa's irritation against her allies were
still at work.   The constant and sometimes imperiously-
worded despatches of the English ministers, and the
somewhat injudicious and outspoken language of Sir
Hanbury Williams, who in 1753 was sent to Vienna to
insist that the empress should satisfy the ever-rising
demands of the German Electors, strengthened her fixed
belief that the English were acting entirely on motives
of self-interest, and were ready without scruple to exact
from her, for their own purposes, concessions which she
felt it impossible to grant.

Meanwhile, under this somewhat hollow pretence of
friendship for England, an attempt to carry out the
second and vital part of the programme was being
silently made in Paris.   Diplomatic relations with
France had been renewed after the Peace of Aix-la-
Chapelle. The friendly reception afforded to the French
envoy in Vienna had met with no return in Paris,

where marked coldness had met the advances of the
Austrian minister, Mareschal.   It was determined to
try the effect of a more important ambassador.   The
empress, who, in spite of the jealous belittling to which
he was subjected at the hands of the older ministers,
had learnt to place the most profound confidence in
Kaunitz, determined that to the author of the plan
should be entrusted the first attempt at its realisation.
In 1750 Count Kaunitz undertook the embassy to Paris.
His letters and reports give but small indication of
success on any important point.   He speaks of his kind
reception, of his gradual introduction as an esteemed
companion into the highest society of Paris, of the
occasional opportunities which offered themselves of
being useful to the king or to his courtiers, of his
popularity when, somewhat oddly, he made his formal
entry into Paris two years after he had been residing
there, and of his friendly intercourse with Madame de
Pompadour.   But he made no impression when he
urged the king to withdraw his opposition to the election
of Joseph, and he entirely failed in any way to loosen
the close connection with the Prussian king.   Singularly
free from passion in his political views, he was able to
understand the French position ; and, working from his
principle that self-interest alone ruled policy, he confessed that the French were following the course most
advantageous to themselves, and therefore that which
they would be almost certain to continue to pursue.
He seems in fact to have gradually convinced himself
that although the views which he shared with his
sovereign as to the true object of his policy, and even
as to the means by which it was to be reached, were

perfectly correct, they were for the present at least wholly unattainable. Before his embassy closed he seriously recommended a reversion to the old system, and advised that the ties which connected Austria with the Maritime Powers should be continually strengthened. His resourceful mind even suggested to him the possibility of a friendship with Prussia. " In such circumstances," he writes, " what reasonable means of securing our own safety is left, except absolutely to forget the loss of Silesia, to remove all cause of jealousy from the King of Prussia in this direction, and thus to bring him into a general alliance with Austria and the Maritime Powers ? " Nor was such a hope groundless. Frederick's alliance with France had been forced upon him by circumstances. It had not proved very advantageous, and considerably hampered his independence. Nor was its permanence certain. The bitterness caused by his double desertion of their alliance during the late war might easily some day ripen into a wish for revenge. It was notorious that he was chiefly occupied with the desire to secure his Silesian conquests. Safety, independence, unquestioned possession of his conquests would all result from the suggested friendship with Austria.

It is impossible to believe that such a line of policy could, under any circumstances, have found favour with Maria Theresa. But, indeed, an event had occurred which seemed to remove the necessity for its adoption and to facilitate friendship with the House of Bourbon. Unsolicited, the Spanish court had made overtures for a defensive treaty. The suggestion was of course gladly accepted. Side by side with it ran a proposal for a double marriage between the two families of Spain and

Austria. When the convention was finally concluded at
Aranjuez the guarantee contained in it was, according
to the wishes of Spain, confined to the possessions of
either country in Italy. But immunity from assault
on this side was at all events secured, while the very
friendly relations thus established with one of the
great Bourbon Houses could scarcely fail to react
advantageously upon France.

On New Year's Day of 1753 Kaunitz resigned his
embassy to assume a higher place. His work in Paris
was by no means so resultless as it appeared. He had
at least succeeded in ingratiating himself with the king
and with the ministers. And more than this, he had
made himself a welcome guest at the house of Madame
de Pompadour. It is difficult to say how far this was
with design. He does not seem as yet to have attempted
to use his influence with her. Yet he recognised fully
the value of her friendship. "I do not know how it
happened," he writes, "but somehow or other it is true
that the king and Madame de Pompadour and their
circle are much attached to me. All this is no doubt
outside real business, but personal affections of this
sort meanwhile do no harm, and upon occasion may
prove of the greatest importance."

The position which awaited Kaunitz on his return
was nothing less than that of State Chancellor. The
empress had been gradually convinced of the incapacity
of Ulfeldt, the present occupant of the post, but her
extraordinary tenderness for the feelings of those who
had served her had prevented her from getting rid of
him till some opportunity should arise of doing so with
honour and satisfaction to Ulfeldt himself. When the

death of Field-Marshal Königsegg vacated the highest
position about the court, that of *Obersthofmeister* or
Lord Steward, she determined to place Ulfeldt in the
vacant office and summon Kaunitz to return to Vienna
as State Chancellor. It was not without some difficulty
that Kaunitz was induced to accept the offer. His
health was bad, and valetudinarianism was growing on
him ; and he had, or professed to have, a disbelief in his
own powers. However, he ultimately consented to
assume, though nominally only for a time, the conduct
of foreign affairs, for the avowed purpose of making
such changes in the arrangements of the office as should
breathe fresh vigour into the external policy of the
country. There is no probability that either he or the
empress had any intention that his appointment should
be of a temporary character. She had learnt to value
his abilities far too highly, and had found his political
ideas too much in sympathy with her own to allow him
to withdraw. At all events, at the beginning of 1753
Count Kaunitz entered upon the position, which he held
for nearly forty years.

The alteration he desired in the Chancery was at
once carried out. It was one of no slight importance,
for it meant the removal of Bartenstein from his office
of Referendary. The separation from Ulfeldt had been
comparatively easy to Maria Theresa, although in a
literal sense it cost her much. With the liberality
which she always displayed towards her old servants,
and perhaps to free herself from his reiterated complaints, she secured to him an income of 45,000 gulden
and a house, besides paying 160,000 gulden of private
debt. Her separation from Bartenstein was a different

matter. In early life she had felt the warmest gratitude
for his advice and assistance. His advice may not
always have been good, but he had served her con-
scientiously, to the very best of his ability. For many
years all the correspondence with foreign courts had
passed through his hands. His great gift of memory,
the restless activity of his mind, and his unrivalled
facility of expression had given him to the full that
power which not infrequently falls to the lot of the able
permanent secretary. Ostensibly in the hands of the
Chancellor and his colleagues, the whole work of the
foreign office had practically devolved upon Bartenstein.
It was impossible that Kaunitz, intending as he did
not only to keep the policy of Austria in his own
hands, but also entirely to change its direction, should
consent to allow so formidable a rival to remain in
office. The ways of Bartenstein were not his ways.
Though capable of using the most bitter language,
Kaunitz as a rule desired, and especially at the
present time, to keep well with foreign courts. Again
and again he had felt it his duty to remonstrate
with the language of Bartenstein's despatches. With
wide and unprejudiced political views, he disliked his
habit of regarding as a crime all opposition to Austrian
opinion. It became therefore necessary that the
secretary should be removed from his office. But Maria
Theresa showed the value she set on his services by
breaking through the iron limits of aristocratic etiquette,
and finding a place for him in the secret Conference,
never before opened to any but the highest aristocracy.

Although the new Chancellor continued to cherish
secretly his intention of dissolving the treaty between

Prussia and France, and of sooner or later regaining the
lost provinces, his ill success in Paris forced upon him
the belief that the time for such action had not yet
arrived.   He assumed, therefore, an attitude of general
friendliness, and to all appearance directed his efforts
towards the maintenance of peace.   But such an attitude
was not long tenable.   A colonial war, which had arisen
between France and England, threatened to involve the
continent, and the crisis came upon him before he was
prepared for it.   To avoid participation in the war
seemed impossible.   The Austrian Netherlands were
the traditional battlefield on which the quarrels between
England and the Bourbon House were decided.   And if
war was inevitable there appeared no choice but to
strengthen the old system of alliances, and to enter it as
of old, side by side with England.   It was also certain
that the same necessity would be felt, and perhaps even
more strongly, in England, for without an ally upon
the continent action would be impossible.   But though
both countries seemed driven to the maintenance of
friendly relations, there was much irritation on both
sides.   Memories of bitter quarrels, of forced and
humiliating submission, of grudging help, of sharp
words and angry despatches, commercial jealousies
lately increased by the Treaty of Aranjuez, and the
never-ending bickering over the Barrier Treaty, were all
so many obstacles in the way of any cordial friendship.
There was, besides, a fundamental difference between
the two courts, in the light in which they regarded the
alliance.   In England it was the habit to think and to
say that Austria owed a deep debt of gratitude to the
Power which had saved it during the late war, and that

H

the debt of gratitude had not been well paid. In Vienna,
with perhaps a truer vision, men saw that under the
guise of friendship England had pursued its own
interests, and that such sacrifices as had been made had
in fact led only to the constant aggrandisement of the
English power. Each nation was filled with a strong
conviction of the selfishness of its ally.

After the conclusion of the peace, the main question
round which this mistrustful feeling had centred was
the Barrier Treaty. This treaty, as originally conceived,
had formulated the conditions on which after the Peace
of Utrecht (1713) the maritime allies had consented to
restore the Low Countries to the House of Austria. That
the provinces should be employed as a bulwark against
the advance of France was an accepted principle; but
the conditions were of a character which necessity alone
could have induced Austria to accept. That the barrier
towns should be occupied by foreign troops under their
own commanders, even though the general supremacy of
Austria was allowed, and that the duty of supporting
the troops should be laid upon the Low Countries, was
an evident diminution of its sovereign rights. Still
more offensive was the selfish policy which revived and
confirmed the restrictions on the trade of the provinces
which it had been thought necessary to impose at the
Treaty of Westphalia (1648). As a matter of fact, the
conditions of the Barrier Treaty had been neglected
on the one side, and carried out in all their severity on
the other. Every restriction upon the commercial independence of the provinces had been upheld; but the
fortresses had been allowed to fall into ruins, garrison after
garrison had retired during the late war without striking

a blow, and some of the fortresses which had been razed
by the French in their invasion were still left unrepaired.

So keen-sighted a man as Kaunitz, who had held the
post of minister plenipotentiary at Brussels before the
Peace of Aix-la-Chapelle, could not fail to be struck
with the evils of the Barrier Treaty; nor could a high-
minded ruler such as Maria Theresa, with the good of
her subjects deeply at heart, forbear to set on foot some
measures for the restoration of their prosperity. She
had therefore indignantly refused to wring from them
the arrears of payment due, which she well knew
would not be employed in the legitimate object of
repairing the fortresses; and she had attempted to raise
the industry of the people by a protective tariff, the
only means at that time recognised. The Maritime
Powers were touched to the quick by this assault upon
their commercial interests. A standing quarrel had
thus arisen. While one party complained that the
subsidies for the maintenance of the fortresses were
unpaid and that tariffs had been established which
destroyed their commercial advantages, the other
party pointed to the absolute neglect of those military
duties which were the very object of the treaty, the
emptied garrisons, and the ruined walls, and indignantly
repudiated the supposition that the provinces were not
held by the Austrian crown in full sovereignty. The
position taken up by the Maritime Powers was peculiarly
irritating to a ruler of the character of Maria Theresa.
The attempted assault on what she considered her
sovereign rights roused her strong indignation. The
outburst of anger with which she received the assertion
of this principle, when made by Sir Hanbury Williams,

was so vehement, he says, as to have been distinctly heard in the neighbouring rooms.

When the two countries both began to think of re-establishing the friendship which had been cooled by these quarrels, it was naturally on this question that the negotiations turned, especially as the defence of the Netherlands was the most obvious point at issue. The English asserted that the best means to fulfil the treaty were the immediate payment of the arrears and the removal of the obnoxious tariff. The empress did not contradict them, but her view of the fulfilment of the treaty was not quite the same as theirs. If the treaty was maintained, it must be for the purpose of securing its original object. In order that Holland might be defended, she was willing to pay the arrears, if the money was honestly devoted to the repair of the fortresses, and if England and Holland would make considerable additions to the troops occupying the provinces. But the destruction of the trade of her subjects she could not allow. She therefore insisted upon the conclusion of a favourable commercial treaty within the year. It speaks well for her desire to retain the friendship of England that she brought herself to yield thus far. She was willing even to go a step further, and to assist in covering Hanover from French assault, if England would undertake the reciprocal duty of the defence of the Netherlands.

The reply of the English ministers was not conciliatory. They would be responsible for no additional expenses ; and, in a despatch which did not spare either threats or complaints, they demanded that an immediate reinforcement of 25,000 troops should be sent to the

Low Countries. Was it possible any longer to bear with allies so unfriendly and so blind to their own interest? Had not the hour arrived for renewing the effort to realise the change of policy? Both Kaunitz and the empress at the moment desired peace. He himself says that he regarded the war as untimely; with designs on Prussia ever in the background, he was not yet prepared for them.

But the despatch required an answer. On June 12, 1755, a sitting of the Conference was held in the presence of the empress, and arguments were urged on both sides of the question. It was plain, they said, that the war was not of Austria's seeking, nor could its conduct depend upon disputes on the other side of the globe. But the fact remained that the French army lay ready for immediate advance upon the Netherlands, and if the frontier was crossed, the war would be actually begun. Nothing was more likely to precipitate the movement of the French army than the knowledge that 25,000 Austrians were marching to make common cause with their enemy. Long before the reinforcements could cover the long journey, the Low Countries would be overrun; and meanwhile the opportunity for which Frederick was watching would have occurred, and the hereditary dominions, stripped of troops, would lie a ready prey before him. On the other hand, it was urged that if the war was inevitable, it was of little import- ance whether the French were irritated or not; and though it must be confessed that the Maritime Powers, busy on the other side of the world with their own interests, would give but little help to Austria, they were still its only allies and it was impossible to stand alone.

Moreover, traditional ties could not be easily broken. Leaving out of sight the probability that the destruction of England meant the destruction of Austria also, it was incompatible with national honour to desert so old a friend.

Kaunitz listened to the arguments, and suggested a compromise. Let Austria send 10,000 men, and let England do the same. But while determining upon this answer, he thought it impossible to pass over in silence the threatening and injurious language of the late communication. In the despatch which he wrote he allowed his feelings free play. England, he said, had always treated the Netherlands as its own property. For more than forty years the voice of righteousness had been hushed in order that the Maritime Powers might wring their own advantage from the wretched provinces. But now, after they had habitually treated them as their own, no sooner did danger arise than they clamoured for the empress to come and save them. She had done her duty. She had offered to leave the defence entirely in the hands of England and Holland, and had placed the army already in the provinces at their disposal. But what had her allies done? Holland had been allowed to withdraw its troops from the barrier towns, and was even now thinking of neutrality. While confining itself to a few treaties of subsidies, England was throwing all the burden of the actual struggle upon Austria. The empress had firmness enough to reject such selfish policy. Nevertheless she was prepared, for the sake of old friendship, to send 10,000 men. More she could not and would not spare; this was positively all that she would do.

It is difficult to resist the impression that Kaunitz intended, by so hotly expressed a letter, to precipitate a breach with England. Yet this does not seem to have been the case. In a memorandum which he immediately afterwards addressed to the empress, he gave her to understand that his despatch was what he called a "touch-stone" to prove the real intentions of England. He still wished, he said, to keep up for the present his old friendships, and the letter could do nothing but good. It was necessary for Austria to assert itself. If the conscience of England was touched by his words, it would enter more actively than before into the war on the side of the alliance. If it took umbrage at it, it would either make peace with France and the war would end, or in its anger turn towards Prussia. It was likely enough that Frederick might refuse the overture, and England would be driven back, humbled, to Austria. If, on the other hand, Prussia welcomed it, the dissolution of the connection between Frederick and France, which Austria had so long desired, must take place of itself. The action of Austria thus rested for the time entirely upon the course pursued by the English court. But although this despatch may not have been so intended, it was in fact the immediate cause of that change in European relations which had so long been in the air. The reply of the English ministry ignored the Chancellor's complaints, and, assuming the permanence of existing relations, put forward certain categorical questions; a form which in diplomacy always bears a threatening aspect. The empress was asked to state what help she was ready to furnish to cover Hanover, and to what expense she would go to raise and pay

auxiliary troops. And, as though the form itself were
not sufficiently threatening, an intimation was given
that, failing satisfactory replies, a treaty of neutrality
would be at once contracted with Prussia. With somewhat insulting irony, it was suggested that such a treaty
would leave the empress at liberty to use all her troops
against the common enemy, France.

There was still a moment of uncertainty during
which the Austrian court thought to meet neutrality by
neutrality. But when the French actually invaded the
Netherlands such thoughts were laid aside, and the
great plan of Kaunitz, which had so long lain dormant,
sprang into life. To realise it in time of peace had
proved impossible, but now in the midst of war the
opportunity seemed to have arrived, and it seemed probable that the French would no longer scruple to accept
the Austrian friendship and thus diminish the number
of their enemies. France at peace with Austria would no
longer require Prussian assistance to create a diversion
in its favour. The uses of the alliance having thus
disappeared, the alliance itself would in all probability
disappear also, and Frederick, left without a continental
ally, would be unable to take any hostile step.

True to his view of the sovereign power of self-
interest, Kaunitz took care in the instructions he sent
to Stahremberg, his successor in Paris, to emphasise the
advantages that would accrue to France from the alliance.
The French desire to find a good settlement for Don
Philip, the king's son-in-law, might be gratified in the
Netherlands: the French candidate for the Polish
throne, the Prince of Conti, might be supported: an
overwhelming alliance, including France, Spain, Naples,

Russia, and Austria, might be called into existence. To
prove the good faith of the empress, Nieuport and
Ostend might be lodged in French hands during the
continuation of the war; and the allies of France—
Sweden, Saxony, and the Palatinate—might revel in
the spoils of a dismembered Prussia. And all that was
asked from the French in exchange was the renunciation
of an alliance with the Prussian king who had already
so often played them false, and the payment of a few
subsidies. If Russia could be induced to move, the
hope of increased dominion would certainly secure the
co-operation of the smaller German states, and make
them the active agents in the assault on Prussia.
Without striking a blow, France would win objects
which a triumphant war could scarcely secure. To
these arguments, there was added, in an abstract which
Stahremberg was empowered to communicate to the representative of the French king, the somewhat strange
assertion that the empress had reason to believe that
England was attempting to approach the Prussian king
through the intervention of the Protestant courts for
the purpose of thwarting the interests of Catholicism, as
well as those of the Houses of Bourbon and Austria. It
would almost seem as if the conscience of the empress
shrank from the somewhat cynical plan of her minister,
and that she sought to stifle her compunctions by
resting her action upon high religious grounds. That
the plan suggested was really a conspiracy against
Prussia is obvious. France was only asked to supply
money to be used in securing the friendship of Russia,
which with the smaller hungry states was to do the
work of dismemberment.

Kaunitz now reaped the fruit of all the trouble he
had taken to make himself agreeable during his Parisian
embassy; he had so far ingratiated himself with Madame
de Pompadour that he felt confident of obtaining direct
access to the king's ear.   And as the political weakness
of Louis XV. was his love of diplomacy and the pleasure
he found in carrying on the higher politics without
reference to his ostensible ministers, there was a fair
prospect that insinuations through so favourable a
channel would receive attention.   Two days after the
receipt of his instructions, Stahremberg betook himself
to the mistress, as the bearer of a letter from the
Austrian chancellor, and begged for an interview with
some confidential person to whom he might safely
communicate matters of the highest importance.   The
person selected was the Abbé de Bernis, a favourite
of Madame de Pompadour, and to him the plan was
communicated in the little country house of La Babiole
in the park of the lady's mansion.   But though unquestionably begun with all the mysterious airs of an
intrigue, it was not long before some at all events of
the ministers were introduced into the secret.

The first step had thus been taken; the French
king had consented to consider the suggestions of the
Austrian court.   But the negotiations advanced very
slowly.   The French were still reluctant to break with
Frederick, their old ally; they were, in fact, earnestly
engaged in attempting to renew the treaty which bound
him to them, and which was to terminate in March
1756.   Various projects were discussed at La Babiole.
The willingness of France to enter into some treaty
with Austria was ensured; but it did not seem likely

that the arrangement would go further than a treaty of neutrality, coupled at most with a defensive alliance. All this hesitation was suddenly brought to an end by the revelation of a treaty between England and Prussia which had been signed at Westminster in January 1756.

Frederick had been watching the course of events with that perfect indifference as to existing ties which characterised his statesmanship. He was determined to take the course which he believed to be most advantageous to himself. He felt indignant at the airs of superiority assumed by his great ally, who treated him somewhat as England treated Austria. The French view, he tells us, seems to have been that "the King of Prussia was to them what the ruler of Wallachia is to the Porte; that is, a subordinate prince, who the moment he receives orders is obliged to make war." The position of his dominions placed the fate of Hanover in his hands. Lord Holderness, the English minister in Berlin, had therefore approached him, desiring no doubt his active assistance, but contenting himself at first with the proposition that he should join in securing the peace of Germany. Frederick was well informed as to the intrigues of the Austrian court. If he renewed his treaty with France, he would be expected to take part in the attack on Hanover, and the Austrians, Russians, and English would be at once on his hands. But if he joined England, as he was well assured that Russia would adhere to the side of the best paymaster, he expected to find himself in a position to oblige the empress to remain at peace. He therefore accepted the propositions of Lord Holderness, and a treaty to secure the neutrality of Germany was signed. From this, the

Netherlands, the present seat of war, was however
excluded.

The treaty was contracted under the very eyes of the
Duke of Nivernois, who was attempting to renew the
French treaty. Foiled in their diplomacy, and irritated
by a declaration of independence on the part of Prussia
little less than insulting, the French ministers at once
assumed a very different tone towards Austria. It was
no longer necessary for Stahremberg to bring forward
proposals, they now came freely from the other side.
About the middle of February it was explained that
Louis was ready to treat. For the good of Europe and
the Catholic religion, he would enter into friendly
relations with Austria. Whether the treaty should be
drawn in accordance with the first plan of Kaunitz, or
with the project for a general neutrality which the
French court had put forward, was left to be determined ;
but there must be no question on one point—the treaty,
whatever it was, must be reciprocal. It lay with
Kaunitz, for he was practical master of the Vienna
Cabinet, to decide which form of treaty was the most
desirable. He determined not to commit himself. If
his own plan, which he would first attempt to realise,
proved impossible, he would content himself with accepting the suggestions of the French ministry. He therefore began by emphasising the advantages derived by
England from its new treaty of neutrality—the road to
Hanover was now closed, the invasion of England
impossible. While, if France declined to listen to the
advances of Austria, it ran the risk of finding Frederick
added to the number of its enemies. But France had
no longer any thought of declining the Austrian friend-

ship. Starting from the firm principle of reciprocity, the French negotiators proceeded to discuss the propositions which had been laid before them. They raised no difficulties on such outlying questions as the exchange in favour of Don Philip, or the conduct of Austria at the next vacancy of the Polish crown, but when the central point was reached, on which alone the Austrians set much store, the diplomatic battle grew hot. The two parties in the negotiation occupied much the same position. Both were intending to throw over an old ally, who was to be left to the tender mercies of a new friend; but both felt some compunction as to setting their own hand to the destruction of one who had so lately been their friend. Stahremberg tried to induce the French negotiators to see the advantage of a joint attack on Prussia, even though Austria gave nothing in return. He urged that the object of the alliance was to neutralise the Treaty of Westminster, and the best way to secure it was by a general assault on Prussia. The success of such an attempt could be rendered certain only by the co-operation of the Powers on the confines of Prussia, such as Sweden, Saxony, and the Palatinate; and to secure their assistance they must be offered portions of the conquered country. A remnant of honourable feeling made the French shrink from complicity in the underhand scheme against their old ally, but they expressed their readiness to declare open war against him, if with complete reciprocity Austria would pursue a similar line of conduct with a view to the destruction of England.

It was not without difficulty that the two courts, so full of mutual mistrust, came to an agreement. But at

length Austria yielded the point on which France laid
so much stress and pledged itself to reciprocity.   That
is to say, they consented to take active measures against
England if France would take active measures against
Prussia.   The close union was not, however, to become
valid till Silesia and Glatz were again in Austrian hands.
As there was much to be done before that end could be
reached—other States to be called upon for their assistance,
Russia to be bribed or persuaded, a French army to be
collected to occupy Hanover and keep the Protestant
princes in awe, and subsidies to be raised—it seemed
plain that the execution of the active part of the plan
could not take place till late in the following spring.
Meanwhile a treaty of neutrality, and a defensive
alliance, might be at once contracted.

The French ministry were not wholly at one as to
the advisability of the approaching change of system.
It had been chiefly arranged by the Abbé de Bernis,
and by Rouillé the foreign minister, acting unquestionably under the influence of Madame de Pompadour.
Even Rouillé was not without some misgivings, while
it required the intervention of the king himself to overrule the objections of D'Argenson.   At a meeting of
the ministry, however, held on April 19, there was no
overt opposition, and the suggestions of Austria were
accepted.   A defensive treaty and a treaty of neutrality
were to be at once contracted, but only as a preliminary
step.   The more important treaty, of an offensive
character, and incorporating in some way all the
Austrian propositions, was to be immediately set on
foot.   On May 1, at Rouillé's house of Jouy, what is
known as the Treaty of Versailles was actually signed.

This treaty, or rather the two treaties, for it was double in form, were of a defensive character. The first was a contract of neutrality. Austria promised to take no part, direct or indirect, in the present war; France promised to avoid all attempt to involve other Powers in the war, and under no pretence to invade the Netherlands. By the second, a defensive alliance was made. The two monarchs promised the mutual defence of their possessions in Europe, and pledged themselves, in case of an assault, to come to the assistance of their ally with 24,000 men. The present war was excluded from the action of this treaty. Certain secret articles followed, by one of which it was stipulated that, in spite of the exception just made, if any French province was attacked by the troops of any other Power than England, calling themselves auxiliaries, Austria should supply its promised troops. The same clause applied to France. As no Power except Prussia was likely to attack an Austrian province, the clause in fact meant that in the case of any hostile movement on the part of Frederick, the assistance of French auxiliary troops might be demanded. By a second clause, the Powers to be admitted to a share in the treaty were regulated. They were confined to the princes of the Bourbon House, and such others as should be admitted by the mutual consent of the contracting parties.

Immediately after the signature and ratification of the Treaty of Versailles, a communication was made to the Austrian ambassador, which explains clearly the temporary character of the present arrangement. "In order to keep up the friendship between the Powers, it is necessary that without delay they should come to

an understanding upon preliminaries to form the basis
of the real secret treaty. The defensive treaty staves
off the immediate danger, the treaty which is to be
contracted looks to the future." In fact, Kaunitz had
won his point, although the actual completion of the
offensive alliance was delayed for a year.

The inevitable intricacies of diplomacy, especially
when employed on so vast a scale, are apt to overlay
the well-marked outline of the historic fact. The whole
story is a lesson on the danger of alliances. The leaders
of Europe were England and France, and the great
question at issue was to which of the two the supremacy
of Europe should fall. There was nothing in their
quarrel which need have implicated the other European
Powers. There was indeed every reason why Germany
should wish to exclude foreign influence from the Empire,
and the King of Prussia had more than once given signs
of his disapproval of intrusive foreign influences. But
the network of treaties was so close that it could be
properly called a system; Europe was divided into
two well-marked groups of close friends under the flag
of one or the other of the two leading Powers, with
whom their interests were supposed to be indissolubly
connected. It was therefore impossible that any war
should arise without the greatest risk of its becoming
universal.

Beyond this permanent danger there were other
special causes at work. The bitter animosity existing
between Austria and Prussia could scarcely allow those
countries to remain neutral when a good opportunity for
hostilities occurred, and the possession by Austria of the
Low Countries, the first point of assault, seemed to force

Austria, whether it so desired it or not, to come forward as the ally of England for the mere purpose of defending its own territory. In the same way the possession of Hanover by the English king, and its close proximity to Prussia, seemed likely to oblige that country also to engage in the war. The binding character of the ties of alliance was at the time regarded as so strong that England and France respectively relied, without any misgiving, on the support of Austria and Prussia. Looking upon themselves as being unquestionably the chiefs of the alliance, they both adopted a tone of superiority, which, as it proved, was exceedingly unwise. The King of Prussia was not inclined to be treated, as he himself says, as "a subordinate prince, who must fight whenever he received orders." Maria Theresa and her minister Kaunitz had long been smarting under English haughtiness, and, as the minister declared, "the empress was too high-minded and clear-sighted to follow blindly the selfish policy of her great ally." It thus happened that the two German monarchs who were expected to serve as auxiliaries in the quarrel, having no interest in common with the principals, and having besides a very grave private quarrel of their own, naturally thought either of securing for themselves and for Germany a neutrality which should localise the war, or the means of satisfaction of their own separate interests if they consented to join in the struggle.

But the Western Powers do not seem at first to have realised this situation, and when Kaunitz opened his negotiations with France, his friendship was at once welcomed, but on the supposition that it would add Austria and such allies as could be brought with her, in-

I

cluding Prussia, to the French alliance. In the same
way, when England approached Prussia, there was no
thought of an entire breach with Austria, and the conclusion of the Treaty of Westminster was explained at
the Austrian court as being of great value to the alliance,
because it healed for the time the private quarrel which
was hampering the empress, and allowed her to turn all
her strength against France. In taking this view the
Western Powers entirely ignored the wounded feelings of
their German allies, and very gravely underrated the
strength of the mutual animosity by which they were
inspired. To Maria Theresa, war meant only an
opportunity for obtaining by a French alliance freedom
of action and assistance in the destruction of Prussia.
Frederick believed he saw in his rejection of the French
alliance an opportunity for that independence which
he particularly valued, and a support from England
and Russia sufficiently strong to secure him from Maria
Theresa's designs, with which he was fully acquainted.

The conclusion of the Treaties of Westminster and
Versailles, which were at first merely defensive, produced the result, which probably the statesmen foresaw,
but which was not ostensibly put forward, of a complete
reversal of the European system, for they both speedily
grew into close offensive alliances.

If the conduct of the empress in her desertion of
England is open to blame, it can only be on the ground
that alliances must be permanent and the interests of
certain countries indissolubly connected. There was
nothing in the nature of things to prevent her from
changing her friends, and there was much in her position
which rendered the change politic. Her answer to

Keith, the English ambassador, is full of good sense, and completely justifies her action, as far as her breach with England is concerned. She traced her inability to make any great effort for the preservation of the more distant parts of her dominions to the conduct of England in obliging her to resign Glatz and Silesia. Not only had Prussia been thereby strengthened, but the feeling aroused on both sides had rendered that country her permanent enemy. Her hereditary provinces were thus threatened on both sides by Prussia and the Porte ; and to defend the centre of her empire was her first duty.

Had she confined herself merely to a treaty of neutrality with France, or kept to her declaration that any accommodation with that country would certainly not be directed against England, her conduct could be open to no blame. Unfortunately, the necessities of alliance as then understood carried her much further than this. Against her will, and in opposition to her feeling of what was right, she was driven into active hostilities with her former ally, and to a violent reversal of policy which it is hard to defend.

CHAPTER VI

CHANGE OF THE SYSTEM OF ALLIANCES (*continued*)

1756-7

THE exclusion of the Low Countries from the benefit of
the Treaty of Westminster was practically a hostile step
against Austria, for it enabled England, while its own
Hanoverian possessions were preserved from assault, to
insist that the Austrians should participate in the war.
The Treaty of Versailles acted in exactly the opposite
direction ; while allowing the French to enter Hanover,
it removed from the Imperial court the responsibility of
the defence of the Low Countries.   The secret clauses of
the treaty paralysed the action of Prussia ; or, should
the king prefer to move, the *casus foederis* arose, and
the French auxiliary troops might be summoned.   It
was no doubt, even apart from the more important
treaty which was in view, a great diplomatic triumph
for Kaunitz.   Without conceding any advantage to the
French, he had secured their participation in an attack
on Prussia should Frederick take immediate action ;
while it was understood to be only a first step to
a treaty of a wider scope which would enable him

to demand their co-operation even in aggressive movements.

Negotiations for such a treaty were at once set on foot. To the honour of France it must be said that its ministers showed much unwillingness to join in a scheme for stripping the King of Prussia of any part of his hereditary possessions. They fought hard to limit their obligations to assistance in recovering the Silesian provinces; on this point, however, Kaunitz and his mistress were absolutely determined. The decision was for a while suspended, and the question was yet pending when its solution became unnecessary; for the action of the Prussian king had supplied all that was wanted to set the already existing defensive treaty in motion.

There is no doubt that the secrets of the Austrian court had been betrayed. Frederick was aware that the hope of Russian assistance which had induced him to sign the Treaty of Westminster was fallacious. With some difficulty the English Parliament had been induced to accept a treaty which, in accordance with the old system of alliances, was to purchase by large subsidies the assistance of the Czar against Prussia. To meet the national feeling which was beginning to set strongly in Frederick's favour, the ministry had been obliged to allow certain modifications in the proposed treaty; the troops, for whose support the subsidies were ostensibly given, were to be employed only in the Low Countries or in defence of Hanover. In this form the treaty was sent over to Russia for ratification. The Russian minister, Bestuchef, well bribed by England, used all his influence in its favour. But the Austrian ambassador was also busy in St. Petersburg, working successfully upon

the implacable hatred to Prussia felt by the Czarina;
and induced her, before she would give her consent, to
insist upon alterations which practically changed its
whole meaning. In its revised form, the troops subsidised
were not to be used either in the Low Countries or in
Hanover. In other words, the assistance which the
English ministry had sought to secure against France
could be only directed against Prussia. The ratification
was still incomplete when the Treaty of Westminster
was contracted; the effect upon Elizabeth, who thus
found her expected prey snatched from her, was immediately seen. No persuasion on the part of the
Austrian ambassador was any longer necessary, she
was only too eager to rush to arms. It was to restrain
her, and so to allow time for the ripening of his great
plan, that Kaunitz had now to exert all his argumentative
powers. For the time, she was satisfied with bringing
together a large body of troops upon the frontier.

Frederick, thoroughly informed of the plans of his
adversaries, knowing that he had nothing to fear till
the following spring, was debating with himself the
propriety of forestalling their attack, and meanwhile
placed his army in favourable positions for immediate
use. In pursuance of the deep-laid plan, the Austrian
court had hitherto kept their troops somewhat osten-
tatiously dispersed; but Frederick's movements seemed
so threatening that they felt compelled to make a
corresponding concentration. The king, who had now
made up his mind, at once took advantage of this step.
He instructed Klinggräf, his minister at Vienna, to ask
for a direct answer to the question whether war was
intended. But it was not to be supposed that Maria

Theresa or Kaunitz would give a direct answer to such
a question. She granted the audience which Klinggräf
demanded, and, as she herself says, dismissed him with
few words. "The critical state of affairs has led me
to think," she said, "those measures necessary which
I am taking for my own safety and for the defence of
my allies, and which have no object beyond this, and
are intended to injure no one." Considering that the
negotiations for the attack on Prussia in the following
year were far advanced, and that the arrangements with
the Russian court had already been completed, this
reply does not seem very close to the truth. But the
empress allowed herself to go still further in the direction
of prevarication. Unsatisfied with this reply, Frederick
instructed his envoy to repeat the question. He explained that he knew that an attack was to be made
upon him in the following year, that an offensive treaty
with Russia had been concluded, that it was true the
assault had been postponed because the troops were not
ready, but postponed only, not given up. "I must
know," he wrote, "whether we are at peace or at war.
Of that the empress is arbiter. I cannot, however, put
up with any oracular answer. If such is given me, the
empress is answerable for the consequences." This time
the question was put into writing, in a document
practically incorporating Frederick's despatch. Kaunitz
in his reply emphasised the threatening preparations of
the king, and the rudeness of the lately communicated
document. "It was impossible," he said, "to answer such
a paper without expressions of unseemly indignation.
The empress was, however, willing to declare that the news
of an offensive treaty between her and Russia, as well

as the suggested conditions of this alliance, were false
and merely invented. No such treaty against Prussia
exists, or had existed." In words this was true, but in
words only. The empress was waiting for an answer
from France, as to what subsidies it would give, before
she formally concluded her Russian treaty.

With the fullest sympathy and admiration for
Maria Theresa, it is impossible not to recognise the
deterioration her character had suffered from the un-
bridled indulgence of her implacable dislike to Frederick.
Such a man as Kaunitz, a cold politician, without
scruples, and resting his political creed wholly upon the
overmastering powers of self-interest, was not the best
adviser for her. It is pitiful to see the noble woman, who
had some years before refused to yield an inch of ground
because she thought that by doing so she was acting
inconsistently with her duty to preserve uninfringed
those rights which she had summoned her allies to
preserve, gradually lowering herself to co-operation in
what was nothing less than a nefarious conspiracy, sink-
ing to prevarication which was scarcely less than false-
hood, and attempting to excuse herself in her own eyes
by throwing over her action a futile veil of religion.
The greatest trouble, Kaunitz tells us, which he found in
carrying out his scheme was to persuade his mistress
that it was right. But he succeeded in so doing. Step
by step her objections were removed. The plea that the
invasion of Hanover was an infringement of the rights
of the empire which she could not allow, disappeared
when set against the invasion of Prussia. The high-
minded assertion that nothing should induce her to
desert her allies was not upheld when the ally made

friends with her enemy. The opportunity offered to
her of healing the ills of Germany by admitting Prussia
frankly to the general alliance was repudiated with
scorn. And she did not think it beneath her to contract
a treaty of neutrality with the object, avowed to her
immediate surrounding, of blinding the eyes of the
courts of Europe till she had ripened her secret plans
for the entire destruction of her enemy.

It was on August 18 that Frederick's memorandum
was given to the empress. On August 25 he received
her answer, and on the next morning he gave orders to
his troops to march. The world was somewhat taken
aback when, instead of entering Bohemia, they marched
upon Saxony. It is this, more than all else, which is
laid to his charge. For Saxony was at peace with him,
and, in its constant fear of so uncomfortable a neighbour,
had avoided the renewal of the treaty of 1746, which
implied the dismemberment of Prussia, and had refused,
since the Peace of Aix-la-Chapelle, to enter into definite
arrangements hostile to Frederick. Thus, even those
authors who are not unwilling to allow that he had a
fair excuse for attacking Austria, point, as a characteristic proof of his rapacious nature, to this unexpected
assault on his peaceful neighbour. It is not perhaps
necessary to pass moral judgments upon the conduct of
personages who fill the scene of history, and perhaps it
is unusually superfluous to do so in the present instance,
though many volumes have been written to decide the
respective guilt of the empress and the king in the
first stage of the Seven Years' War. The animosity
between Austria and Prussia was so highly strung that
a war within some short space of time was inevitable;

whether it came earlier or later was really of little
moment. Nor were the rulers on either side scrupulous
in their conduct. Yet it must be confessed that in
making his sudden inroad upon Saxony, Frederick had
large justifications. If it be certain that France and
Austria had combined in a distinct conspiracy against
him ; that they had sought and obtained the co-operation
of Russia, although the treaty was not actually signed ;
that a part of their arrangement was the dismemberment
of his kingdom, and the satisfaction of the allies of France
—among whom Saxony was included—with the dismembered fragments ; that Saxony, although its Elector
and ministers had shrunk from any direct conventions
on the subject, had been informed by the St. Petersburg
court of the intended action ; that all this was perfectly
well known to Frederick through his agents and spies ;
but that at the same time, and from the same sources,
information had been given him that the assault had been
postponed for a year ; it would surely have been an inconceivable act of folly had he held his hand and quietly
awaited the consummation of the plot against him.

The possibility of an irruption into Bohemia had
been all along contemplated by the Austrian ministers,
and considerable forces had been collected on the Eger
and in the neighbourhood of Königgrätz. The line of
march adopted by Frederick was, however, a surprise.
A hurried conference was assembled at the house of
Kaunitz ; Marshal Browne and General Piccolomini
were sent off at once to assume the command of their
respective armies, and to give assistance to the Saxon
Elector. Two considerable bodies of troops had been
brought together, but not without difficulty ; especially

from Hungary had the supply of men fallen short. In spite of what is so frequently asserted as to the loyalty of the Hungarians, their assistance was always grudgingly rendered, and the price paid for it high. In the present instance, the request for troops or money was met by the old complaint that the exit to their productions was closed by the high tariffs of the Austrian states. Even the Palatine Louis Esterhazy gave the empress to understand that some concession on the point would be necessary. She could not bring herself to yield; and it was chiefly through the loyalty of certain individual nobles that any reinforcements were obtained.

If the advance of the king through Saxony had been a surprise, still greater was that caused by the action taken by the Elector. Instead of falling back upon Bohemia and forming a junction with Browne's army, he determined to throw his troops, some 18,000 in number, into the camp at Pirna, which he believed to be unassailable. He was rapidly surrounded by Frederick's forces. All that Browne could do was to press forward in hopes of arranging some plan to allow of the escape of the beleaguered army. This movement brought on the first battle of the war. Frederick pushed forward to meet the advancing Austrians, and encountered them at Lobositz (October 1, 1756). The contest was not very decisive. In Vienna, indeed, it was regarded as a victory, and was honoured with rejoicings; but Browne had to withdraw from the field, and to confine himself to an ineffectual effort to bring a small body of troops to the assistance of the Saxons. The movement entirely failed. The Saxon army was beaten back as it attempted to cross the Elbe, and was compelled to surrender. All formal opposition on the part of Saxony was thus removed, although many of the Elector's troops played a somewhat brilliant part in the ensuing war.

The occupation of Dresden and Saxony appeared to satisfy the Prussian king, who had now secured a direct opening into Bohemia and removed the scene of future war outside his own dominions. He withdrew for the present into Silesia, and permitted the Elector to retire in peace to his Polish capital.

Meanwhile the conspirators at Vienna were busy with their treaties. Although not exactly at their own time, Frederick had done what they wanted. By taking the initiative in the war, he had, at all events, called into activity the defensive alliances already contracted. With regard to France there arose an immediate difficulty as to how the defensive Treaty of Versailles should be carried out. The French were eager to go much beyond their bargain, and to advance with a large army through Hanover to the western frontier of the Prussian king. Maria Theresa, on the other hand, demanded only the promised succour of 24,000 men, and desired that, strictly as auxiliaries, they should join her troops in Saxony. She was not, in fact, as yet ready to complete the breakup of her old system of alliances, nor could she without some compunction acquiesce in so immediate a breach of the convention of neutrality which had accompanied the treaty, or the introduction of the French army and French influence into the heart of the German Empire. It excites no surprise that her sensitive mind should have felt such scruples. But it is scarcely possible to credit Kaunitz with honesty when we find him, in his despatches to Stahremberg, writing as though he still

believed in the existence ,of the old alliances, and
urging them as arguments in opposition to the French
plan for the assault on Hanover.

After some discussion, matters advanced so far that
the Count d'Estrées was sent to Vienna for the purpose of
arranging a joint plan of operations. It was then that the
difficulties of the defensive treaty, and its want of reality
in the absence of any common interest between the two
contracting parties, became apparent. D'Estrées urged
the view of his court that the French assistance should
assume the form of a large army advancing into Hanover.
The reply of Kaunitz was in favour of a far smaller
French force, brought through Swabia and the Voigt-
land, to serve with the Austrians in Saxony. He
supported this view by pointing out both the danger
and inefficiency of such a movement as the attack upon
Hanover. It would break the treaty of neutrality and
destroy all hope of localising the war, while affording
no real help to Austria. For it was certain that England
would not neglect such an opportunity for generalising
the war in its own interests ; it was even possible that
the Protestant princes might see in the movement an
act of Catholic aggression, and that the introduction of
all the bitterness of religious hostility would be the
consequence. To overcome this opposition might be
within the power of France, but it would certainly be a
matter of time, and would prevent the immediate assistance wanted by the Austrian court. More than this,
England, not yet actually free from treaty connection
with the empress, would at once break loose from these
ties and ally itself with her enemies, and perhaps even
excite the Turks, the ever-threatening foe of Austria,

to active hostility. On the other hand, the Austrian
proposition allowed of the passage of the troops through
Austrian or imperial territory, and therefore without
breach of neutrality; their small number and declared
character of auxiliaries would prevent the German
princes from taking fright and having recourse to arms;
France, which had already been successful in the Mediterranean, would be able to give a good account of its
English enemy; and as the frontier towards the
Netherlands would be in friendly hands, there would be
no risk of that general war which had more than once
proved disastrous to France in its contest with England.   Thus Austria with its Russian allies and its
French auxiliaries, at peace with all the world besides,
would be left to cope in its own fashion with its
Prussian neighbour.   All that was necessary would be
a French army of observation on the lower Rhine,
to impose upon its enemies and to support its friends
among the German princes.

The arguments had only one failing, they rested on
the hollow supposition that England and Hanover
would remain calm spectators while the empress and her
Russian ally destroyed the Prussian king.   Maria Theresa
did not appear to see, and Kaunitz did not choose to
see, that the alliance with France would inevitably be
construed as a desertion of friendship with England.
They preferred to be regarded as aiming at a general
neutrality, and even went so far as to demand help from
George as one of the guarantors of the Pragmatic
Sanction and the Treaty of Breslau.   It would seem to
have been the object of Kaunitz, by posing as the
honest upholder of general neutrality, and as being

engaged only in taking necessary steps for the preservation of Austria against Frederick the self-willed breaker of the peace, to gain time for the completion in the following year of his real projects of vengeance.   There was, in fact, a complete unreality about the whole of these negotiations; for offensive alliances, both with France and Russia, were at the very time being hotly pressed.   In the pursuit of these two treaties similar difficulties were encountered.   In both instances the claims of the allies whose assistance Kaunitz was seeking had to be moderated, lest Austria should find that it was paying too high a price for their friendship and carrying off too small a share of the prospective advantages.

An additional obstacle was found in the jealous wakefulness with which every nation watched the possible increase of its neighbour.   The diplomatic inventiveness of the Austrian minister was sorely tried; but, as he was hampered by no scruples, his ingenuity contrived to find inducements for both parties.   The Czarina had demanded the provinces of Courland and Senegalia.   According to the received principles of the time, Austria could not allow so large an increase to the power of Russia without claiming a corresponding advantage for itself.   Moreover, Courland owned the supremacy of the Polish crown.   It therefore occurred to Kaunitz that the kingdom of East Prussia, not long since in a similar position, might be taken from Frederick, replaced in its dependence upon Poland, and settled in perpetuity upon an Austrian archduke. Satisfaction would thus be given to the Czarina, the Polish king would not be alienated, and the empress

would obtain an excellent settlement for one of her
younger sons. But such a treaty must be kept pro-
foundly secret; for the interests of France in the
east of Europe by no means allowed a great increase
of Russian dominion; its interest in Germany did not
allow of any great accession of strength to Austria, even
though it was its ally, nor of too great a diminution of
Prussia, although it was its enemy. A characteristic
plan was devised. The newly-established relations with
France forbade that the treaty should be kept entirely
secret from it; an appearance of perfect frankness was
necessary. In order that Maria Theresa might with
scrupulous regard to truth assert that there were no
secret clauses, she expressed her willingness that all the
arrangements with respect to Courland and East Prussia
should be embodied, not in a treaty, but in a declaration
mutually signed by the two empresses. The eagerness
of the Russians to get into action enabled her eventually
to spare herself this poor prevarication. The understanding existed, but was not reduced to writing, and
the Convention of St. Petersburg was finally contracted
in February 1757, by which each empress promised to
supply 80,000 troops, and not to make peace till Prussia
had been destroyed, at the same time securing to the
Elector of Saxony a satisfactory indemnity, in the
neighbourhood of Magdeburg, for the insults heaped
upon him.

A few months later, in May, exactly a year from the
signature of the Treaty of Versailles, the negotiations
with France were also brought to a successful issue.
The diplomatic struggle had been of a more intricate
and difficult character. No doubt each of the contract-

ing powers had something to complain of in the conduct
of one or other of the newly allied nations against which
their arms were henceforward to be directed.   Maria
Theresa was smarting under losses which she attributed
to her old overbearing ally, England.   France recollected
with bitterness that on more than one occasion it had been
deserted at critical moments by the Prussian king.   But
there was in truth no common enemy against whom they
could combine.   Traditional feeling and recent animosity
in each case marked out a separate rival.   To France
the destruction of England, to Austria the destruction
of Prussia was everything.   As a matter of course, therefore, the negotiators used all their ability to twist the
treaty they were making to the advantage of their own
peculiar side of the quarrel.   The proposition advanced
by Kaunitz that France should be remunerated for
assisting to restore Silesia and Glatz to Austria, by the
possession of the Netherlands or of some portion of it,
was, roughly speaking, taken as the basis of the treaty.
Coupled with this was the assertion to which France
persistently clung, that complete reciprocity was necessary.   The meaning which was given to the words
"reciprocity and equality of advantage" was the chief
point at issue.   To the French negotiators it meant
quite simply that if they assisted Austria to destroy
Prussia, Austria should assist them to destroy England.
The extent to which this idea was modified in the final
treaty is the measure of the ability of Kaunitz as a
diplomatist.   In the first sketch offered by the French
minister, England was represented as standing side by
side with Prussia in the late breach of treaty, and
therefore requiring similar treatment; the French de-

K

manded, besides the Netherlands, which as both parties
agreed were to be placed in the hands of Don Philip the
French king's son-in-law, the two seaport towns of
Ostend and Nieuport as giving the command of the
channel; they demurred also, and not unnaturally, to
the postponement of the completion of the exchanges
till the empress had effected the spoliation of Prussia.
The Austrian negotiators urged that this was not the
true view of reciprocity.   They had no proof at all that
England had been directly cognisant of Frederick's
action, and could not therefore place it on the same
footing and threaten it with the same vengeance; there
was no concession on the part of France in any way
answering to the surrender of Ostend and Nieuport.
Reciprocity must mean the joint pursuit of certain
objects, coupled with an equality of sacrifice; but the
sacrifices were all on the side of Austria. The surrender
of the Netherlands was a vast political sacrifice entirely
destroying the link which bound Austria to the Maritime Powers; the advantage to France of a safe frontier
was simply enormous; the exchange of the Netherlands
for Silesia, Glatz, and other provinces, when their wealth
and commercial value was considered, was entirely in
favour of France; even in the matter of troops, France
was offering an army of 110,000 men, and for its maintenance 12,000,000 gulden a year, while Austria would
have to put 200,000 in the field, and bear a far greater
expense in maintaining them.

A moment of intense anxiety occurred in the course
of the negotiations when an attempt was made to
assassinate the French king. Had he died, the whole
project might have died with him.   Had he been seri-

ously ill, the remembrance of what had happened in
1741 might well excite fear lest the mistress should be
driven from her position, and with her the chief support
of the Austrian negotiations. But fortune favoured
them. It was almost immediately known that no
such catastrophe was to be apprehended, and that
Madame de Pompadour would resume her influence.
Before long a change of ministry, the disappear-
ance of D'Argenson and Machault to make room for
the Abbé de Bernis, proved the completeness of her
triumph.

When the treaty, completed under the auspices of the
mistress, made its appearance, it was evident that the
diplomacy of Kaunitz had been successful on nearly every
point. The crime of England was not complicity with
Frederick, but refusal to send assistance to Maria Theresa.
It was Prussia alone, and not Prussia and its allies, against
whom efforts were to be directed. The subsidies and
help of France were to be continued till the empress
was in peaceful possession of Silesia and Glatz, of the
Princedom of Crossen, and of some convenient piece of
country in immediate contiguity to her hereditary
estates. The present possessor of that property was
to be remunerated at the cost of Prussia. The war
was not to be closed till Silesia, Glatz, Crossen,
Magdeburg, Halberstadt, Haller, Swedish Pomerania,
and the Prussian inheritance in Cleves were given up.
Then, and not till then, was France to receive certain
fortresses in the Low Countries, including Ostend and
Nieuport, and Don Philip his promised settlement.
Besides all this, France was to use its influence for the
election of Joseph as King of the Romans, to assent to

the establishment of the Archduke Leopold in Modena, and to secure to Austria the reversion of the Netherlands if Don Philip left no heir. On these terms France promised the services of 115,000 men and subsidies of 12,000,000 gulden.

It has been sometimes held that the change of alliances thus introduced was advantageous both to Europe and to France. But in truth it was nothing but a striking and almost incomprehensible success of selfish diplomacy. Though every now and then in his dispatches Kaunitz put forward the advantage of France, it did not in all probability weigh a feather's weight in his calculations. His acute mind had fathomed the weakness of the French Government; the vain pleasure Louis found in dabbling in diplomacy behind the backs of his ministers, his eagerness to secure a settlement for his son-in-law, the determination of the mistress to obtain political ascendency, and the certainty that a novel and striking combination supported by the woman to whom he was slavishly devoted would possess a charm too strong for the king's weak nature to resist. The great diplomatist dangled the bait before the eyes of his victims, and they greedily took it. The wiser French ministers saw the mistake into which they were running. But opposition to the crown was impossible; it was silenced by the king's orders, and when necessary a change of ministers secured obedience. Thus, for no present or permanent advantage — except such as might be supposed to be derived from comparative safety upon the north-east frontier—France suffered itself to be drawn entirely aside from its true interests, to plunge into a war with which it had no concern, and which inevitably secured its failure in a contest which was really vital. At the same time it broke with all the traditions of the policy carefully built up by its greatest statesman, and lost at once its commanding position in Germany, in France, and in Eastern Europe.

For Austria itself, with the appearance of success, the treaty was also disastrous. Not one of the advantages it promised was obtained. Its results were a useless alliance and an abiding enmity, which through many variations of fortune has reached its final issue in our own days. The selfishness of the whole proceeding, the utter disregard of imperial interests, and the bitter hostility established between Austria and North Germany, are practically the roots from which all its subsequent disasters have sprung. But if a gift of insight, which under the circumstances would have been little less than prophetic, be denied to Kaunitz, the brilliancy of his conception, the keen comprehension of the dominant motives of the rulers of the time, the skilful fence and the indomitable firmness he displayed, are worthy of all admiration. Neither he nor the mistress whom he served, and who rewarded him with her fullest confidence, is to be much blamed for failing to recognise the invincible genius of their adversary. If ever sufficient precautions were taken to give the varnish of success to a somewhat questionable action, they were certainly taken on the present occasion. It was impossible to suppose that a little kingdom of some 5,000,000 inhabitants should thwart the projects of the three greatest Powers in Europe.

The assailants, indeed, were not confined to these

three great Powers. Chiefly to prevent the war from
assuming a religious character, though she had herself
used the religious argument to France, the empress
thought it desirable to obtain the support of the
German Empire. At the Diet of Ratisbon, by a
majority in all three colleges, a majority which included a small number of the Protestant states, the
propositions of the empress were approved, and it
was resolved to form what is known as an army of
execution, to bring to reason the disturber of the peace
of the empire. To the command of this army the
Prince of Hildburghausen was appointed. French
and Imperial diplomacy was also active in Sweden,
which was persuaded to join in the' alliance on the
same excuse as that put forward by France, that is to
say, as one of the guaranteeing Powers of the Westphalian Treaty. In the course of the year this convention ripened like the other treaties and took an
offensive form. The reward of Sweden was to be
Pomerania. " With God's help," wrote Kaunitz, " we
will bring so many enemies on the back of the insolent
King of Prussia that he must succumb."

CHAPTER VII

THE SEVEN YEARS' WAR

1757–1760

FREDERICK was not a man to wait quietly till his enemies were upon him. The allies were still busy talking over the plans of the war, and slowly strengthening their armies for the coming campaign, when the Prussians burst in from different directions into Bohemia, and, sweeping all before them, drove the Austrian troops under Charles of Lorraine and Marshal Browne to take refuge within the walls of Prague. A rapid and ably contrived concentration brought the Prussian army within striking distance of them on the hills to the east of the city. A battle fiercely contested, and bloody even among the many battles of that time, resulted in the complete defeat of the Austrians (May 6, 1757). The loss of their able and energetic commander, Browne, threw the sole responsibility upon the weaker shoulders of Prince Charles, and the army was driven backward within the walls. The siege was immediately formed, and all intercourse with the outside world cut off.

News of the disaster, brought by fugitives, met
Kaunitz, who was on his way to consult with the
generals, and was by him carried to the army of
Field-Marshal Daun. It was a frightful blow to the
Austrian court. Their fine-spun plan seemed rent in
fragments; the army of Daun in Bohemia alone stood
between them and the victorious Frederick. But the
high spirit of the empress and of her minister did
not quail. Messages were at once sent to reassure
the hesitating allies, and every measure that was
possible was taken to reinforce and encourage the
army on which the safety of Vienna depended. Daun
was not a man fitted for a rapid stroke of arms, such
as seemed necessary to break through the ring which
surrounded Prague. Yet his peculiar talent, his
excellent discrimination in the choice of position, and
his unceasing care and watchfulness were exactly what
was needed for the other part of his duty, the preservation of Vienna.

The advance of the Austrian army, if somewhat slow,
was too threatening to be overlooked by Frederick.
He at once despatched troops he could ill spare to
make some sort of head against them ; for he hoped
that the speedy capture of Prague would soon release
him and enable him to follow with the rest of his army.
But the Austrians within the city, still 40,000 strong,
were not to be rapidly overcome ; and when certain
information reached him that Daun would in a few
days attempt to join hands with the imprisoned
garrison, Frederick, seeing that there was no time to
be lost, hurried forward after his lieutenant, taking
with him a small reinforcement. The cautious field-

marshal, not unwilling to draw the king farther from
his supports, fell slowly backward, and at length took
up a very strong position in the neighbourhood of
Kolin. Frederick, who always preferred to act on the
offensive, attempted to make up by military genius
for his vast inferiority in numbers. But his great
flank attack, so marked a feature in his tactics, was on
this occasion thwarted, partly by the firmness of the
Austrian troops, partly by the errors of his own
generals, and ended in a disastrous defeat (June 18,
1757).

It is easy to imagine the intense excitement with
which these events were watched in Vienna. The joy
with which the news of the victory of Kolin was
received was proportionate to the depression which
had followed the battle of Prague. Daun became the
hero of the moment, the saviour of his country. The
military "Order of Theresa" was established to cele-
brate the day; and the first cross of the Order was
bestowed on the triumphant general. More time than
enough was wasted by the army in rejoicings. The
agile enemy slipped from their grasp, lost not a
moment in raising the siege of Prague, and retired in
safety towards the Saxon frontier.

This victory put a new face upon the whole proceedings connected with the war. Allies, who had hung
back on the news of the battle of Prague, were ready
enough to strike in when the Prussians had shown that
they were not invincible, and when the Austrians had
given proof that the reforms carried out during the
peace had made their army something very different
from the weak and ill-regulated mass of soldiers it had

been in the previous war. The great plan seemed to
become at once practicable. Frederick saw enemies
closing in upon him on all sides, and was driven to take
the defensive. With his small army it seemed hardly
possible that he should escape annihilation. The
personal dread of him was no doubt extreme; but he
could not be everywhere. Kaunitz—for even in matters
of war his voice was always predominant—was constantly
urging upon Prince Charles and the field-marshal the
necessity of somehow destroying the weak army, which
under the command of Prince Henry lay near them in
the Lausitz, before the king could come to its rescue.

But already the weakness of Austria as a fighting
Power began to show itself. Its army had been greatly
improved; the artillery school had produced excellent
results; the frontier troops when joined with a certain
number of regulars proved invaluable, and in the hands
of Laudon were rapidly earning a foremost place in
military reputation. But a strange want of initiative
appeared to hang over the generals, and to paralyse the
excellent machine which they commanded. It would
seem as if the very greatness of the empress, her strong
personality, and the efforts at centralisation she had so
successfully been carrying out, acted harmfully upon
the character of her generals. They lost much of their
independence, and that readiness to assume responsibility
in critical moments which is essential for the vigorous
prosecution of war. Nor was it wholly advantageous
that the head to whom they looked was a woman.
High-tempered and magnanimous though she was, there
were inevitably times when the weakness of her sex
exerted its effect upon her—she could not rid herself

of strong personal likes and dislikes, and at this very
time, in spite of the very general and well-grounded
belief in his incapacity, she insisted in retaining her
brother-in-law in the chief command. Moreover, the
command thus badly placed was weakly exercised.
Councils of war, though their habitual failure to arrive
at great and vigorous decisions has become a common-
place, were of daily occurrence. Even such decisions
as they arrived at were not regarded as absolute, but
were sent to Vienna for the final decision of the
empress herself. She does not seem to have intention-
ally countenanced this attempt to throw all responsibility
upon the central power. In many of her replies she
expressly pointed out that movements in war must
depend upon the circumstances of the moment. But
the full answers which she gave, the frequency with
which she left the decision in the hands of the majority
of the council, the direct recommendation of certain
lines of action of which she specially approved, all
tended to foster the feeling of dependence, and to
render the action of the army slow and wavering. As
a natural consequence, unaware of what she was doing,
she was frequently displeased with the conduct of the
war, and from herself, or from Kaunitz, objurgations to
more rapid and decisive action were continually reaching
the commanders.

Thus periods of hesitating inaction were followed
now and then by bursts of activity of uncertain wisdom.
After lying in front of the inferior Prussian army so
long that even the emperor thought it necessary to
write to his brother in terms of stinging severity, the
commanders turned upon Silesia. Though they allowed

themselves to be anticipated at Breslau by the Duke of
Bevern, after a while they summoned sufficient determination to fall upon him.   His defeat in a closely
contested battle (November 22, 1757) was immediately
followed by the capture of the city, and by the surrender
of the strong fortress of Schweidnitz.   The aim of all
the Austrian hopes, the reconquest of Silesia, seemed
now an accomplished fact.   The province began again
to be treated as though it was reunited to the Empire.
The inhabitants were absolved from their allegiance to
Frederick ; the position in future of the various religions,
of the nobility and the other classes, was defined ; and
in the enthusiasm of the moment the loud voice of those
who greeted the conquerors was held to prove the desire
of the people to return to their old masters.

The triumph was short-lived.   The king had been
forced to march hurriedly to the west to check the army
of the Empire, and their French allies, who had pressed
on to Erfurt.   His march was for a moment checked
by a sudden stroke resembling but little the usual
methodical proceedings of Austria.   General Haddick,
who had been left behind when Prince Charles had
turned towards Silesia, burst into sudden activity,
dashed northward across the frontier, and, pushing his way between the Prussian forces, occupied a
suburb of Berlin itself.   An unsupported movement of
the kind could produce no great result.   Haddick was
glad to hurry back with an inconsiderable ransom
of £30,000.   But it was an insult which raised the
king's anger, and which was terribly avenged.   Satisfied
that the march upon Berlin was an isolated effort,
he resumed his western operations and at Rossbach

(Nov. 5, 1757) inflicted with his small army a crushing defeat upon the ill-drilled and ill-commanded troops of the Empire and of France. It was a defeat so complete that for the time all hope of renewing the attack in that direction disappeared.

The echoes of Rossbach had scarcely died away when Prince Charles and Daun heard that the terrible king had crossed the whole breadth of his dominions, and was already in their immediate neighbourhood. It might have been wiser to have adopted their old plan, and to have carried on a war of positions. But proud of their success, urged onward by the court, and relying on their superior numbers, they for once decided upon a pitched battle upon equal terms. They drew up their army near Leuthen, covering the roads to Breslau, and there was fought what was in many ways the most decisive battle of the war (December 5, 1757). On this occasion no accidental hindrance interfered with the complete success of Frederick's tactics. The whole strength of his army was thrown upon the left flank of the Austrians, and after a very gallant resistance their army was practically annihilated. Its shattered remnants withdrew at once beyond the Silesian border. The retreat was rendered more difficult by the animosity of the inhabitants, a somewhat striking sequel to the affected joy which had met the Austrian occupation of Breslau.

Neither party in the great struggle had much reason to congratulate itself upon the checkered events of the year. Frederick had shown himself invincible in the field, and apparently capable of bidding defiance to the vast confederation against him; the Russians had done

nothing but capture Memel ; the Swedes had been
forced to retire into their own Pomerania ; the French
had been swept back ignominiously at Rossbach. Silesia
was as far as ever from being reconquered. On the
other hand, Frederick's attempt to penetrate into
Bohemia had signally failed.

Under these circumstances, it was very natural that
thoughts of peace should arise. With all the prestige of
two great victories, yet conscious of the limited nature
of his resources, Frederick considered it a good opportunity for making indirect overtures to France.
Although at first the French king and ministry refused
to acknowledge any feeling of depression, and vehemently
declared their intention of clinging closely to their
Austrian friends, it is certain that the suggestions did
not fall wholly upon unwilling ears. The adoption of
the new policy had produced in France the results which
its supporters desired. Madame de Pompadour and
her friends were triumphant, the old ministers had
withdrawn, and the Abbé de Bernis had succeeded to
the post of foreign minister. But already he had begun
to feel the charge too heavy for him, and to understand
the difference between the irresponsible support of a
great and questionable political change and the responsible duty of carrying it out. The miserable want of
success which had hitherto attended the great combination had forced itself upon his notice, and he was already
turning over in his mind the possibility of deserting
it. In a letter to Stainville, the ambassador at Vienna,
he depicted in the blackest hues the disastrous position
of affairs at present, and the still more disastrous outlook. " I see that in ten or twelve days the Vienna

court has lost three-fourths of its troops and officers,
Russia is selling its artillery horses for a hundred sous
apiece.   Is it possible that the Czarina, in her weakness
and illness, can counteract the plans of Bestuchef, bought
with vast bribes by England?   There is the empress
without an army, and the French ill-disciplined and
without a general, hemmed in between the Prussians
and the Hanoverians.   If I could see generals fit to
command our armies, and a good military council in
Vienna and Versailles, I would not, in spite of our
errors and our common misfortunes, give up the game.
But as I can hope for no change in this respect, and time
is pressing, I give my voice for peace.   If the Austrian
court will let us negotiate, or negotiate with us, we
may get ourselves honourably out of our difficulty.
Meanwhile let us arm ; it is the first step to peace."

Though the French minister declared this to be his
private opinion only, it was hard to believe that he
would speak so openly without the cognisance of the
king.   The letter tended still further to increase the
despondency which the news of the disaster of Leuthen
had excited in the mind of the empress.   Though she
had put a good face on the matter at first, she owns
that in a few days she lost all heart ; and, speaking like
a woman the thoughts which were uppermost in her
mind, she had even betrayed her feelings to the French
ambassador.   At this crisis, the help of Kaunitz was invaluable.   He never for a moment wavered.   He encouraged the ambassador, he encouraged the empress.
He assumed a tone of almost indignant firmness, and when
Stainville suggested that as France could not fulfil the
conditions of the late treaty it had better be dropped, he

replied with unusual warmth that it was not the habit
of the Austrian court to contract a treaty and then at
once to turn its back on it; he rejected absolutely the
suggestions of France, and formally demanded the auxiliary troops and subsidies which had been promised. His
firmness produced the result desired. Indeed Madame
de Pompadour seems always to have been persistent in
her hatred to Prussia, and both minister and king were,
after all, her creatures. The momentary depression of
the empress passed away; Bernis made a sort of
retractation of his views; King Louis wrote with his
own hands a friendly and determined letter. The
negotiation between the courts confined itself to a consideration of the ways and means for carrying on the
war.

The opening of the new campaign, however, was not
such as to strengthen the French in their hesitating acceptance of the wishes of Austria. The command of the
armies in Germany had been entrusted to the Count of
Clermont. He had found himself opposed, no longer by
the incompetent Duke of Cumberland, but by a general of
very different capacity. For Pitt had breathed new life
into the English Government, and, determined to make
the defence of Hanover and the assistance of the Prussian
king a reality, he had obtained from him the services of
Ferdinand of Brunswick as commander of the combined
army. The change was instantaneously felt. The
French armies were unable to retain their position in
Germany, and at the beginning of April had been forced
to withdraw behind the Rhine. Again the French ambassador in Vienna received letter after letter suggesting
the necessity of peace; at most the campaign of the

present year was to be fought with the express purpose of closing with a peace. This was not a mere general suggestion. An outline of the terms on which such a peace might be contracted was given, and the friendly Power who might serve as mediator pointed out. At the same time an earnest wish was expressed that while the war lasted it should be transferred from Silesia to Saxony. Maria Theresa saw with indignation that by the suggested terms Silesia was still to remain in the hands of her enemy. She could not persuade herself that the whole conduct of France was anything else than a false appearance of friendship, intended to cover an already formed determination to contract a separate peace with Frederick. The hasty retirement of Clermont, coupled with the suggestion that she should hold her hand in Silesia and work apparently chiefly for the advantage of the French ally Saxony, drove her to think that she was being made a plaything of the French policy. For a while it seemed really as though it would go hard with Kaunitz's great political achievement. In clear words the empress wrote to him that she thought the war must be carried on entirely irrespective of the French, whose assistance was not worth counting. It was with Russia, she said, that close alliance must be henceforward sought. As a separate alliance with Russia would almost certainly have carried with it a renewed connection with England from which Russia had never formally separated, had the empress's suggestion been adopted, the whole of Kaunitz's great work would have been entirely annihilated, and the political pendulum would have swung back to its old position.

Kaunitz was thoroughly alarmed at the line the

empress was taking. He took elaborate trouble to
prove to her satisfaction the advantages of the new
system. This was not so easy as it was to prove the
disadvantages of the old system. An abiding sense of
injury suffered at the hands of England was one of the
weak points in the political judgment of the empress;
and through this Kaunitz was able to recover her
allegiance to his views, and when Stainville produced,
with his wonted vehemence, the propositions of his
court, she appears already to have been instructed by
her minister to refuse immediate answer, and to declare
the necessity of referring the matter to her council.
Yet her judgment was in fact strictly correct. The
assistance that she received from the French alliance
was of little worth to her; it was from Russia that the
blows came under which Frederick nearly succumbed.
France was not indeed guilty of the double-dealing
which she suspected. The substitution, in the spring
of 1758, of Belleisle for the inefficient war minister who
had hitherto held office, added some vigour to French
action; and when, in the following December, Cardinal
Bernis was removed, and his place taken by Stainville
himself, now become Duke of Choiseul, the friendship of
the two courts was fully renewed. But the exhaustion
of France made it impossible to supply the vast subsidies
to which it was pledged; the new generals proved
inefficient; and the weakness of the administration
deprived the alliance of the expected advantages.

But before this important change of ministers took
place, much of the campaign was over. The empress
had at length summoned courage to remove her incompetent brother-in-law, and had placed the chief command

in the hands of Field-Marshal Daun. Trembling as she always did for her hereditary dominions, she threw all her energy into the strengthening of the army in Bohemia. The campaign which followed affords an excellent illustration of the strongly contrasted abilities of the rival leaders, and of the nicely balanced character of the war. The king again took the initiative. Avoiding the army which had been concentrated in Bohemia to cover Vienna from his expected irruption, he struck straight at the heart of the Austrian Empire, through Moravia which had been largely divested of troops. Again the capital trembled in fear of seeing the enemy before its walls; the fortress of Olmütz alone covered it. But Olmütz proved more difficult of capture than Frederick had expected, and Daun had now found in General Laudon a partner to whom he could entrust those active strokes of war for which he felt himself unsuited. The great distance of Olmütz from his own dominions obliged the king to supply his army and support his siege by successive convoys. As in most cases in which he engaged in siege operations, he trusted much to rapid success; the last convoy was bringing him, as he believed, all that was necessary to secure his purpose, when it was fallen on by Laudon and entirely destroyed. Frederick was compelled to raise the siege; he withdrew, not into Silesia, but into Bohemia, whence he still threatened Vienna. It was then that the peculiar genius of Daun was shown. He refused to allow himself to be forced into a battle, and by a series of skilful manœuvres contrived to drive the king out of Bohemia. But there his success ceased. When Frederick found it necessary to take in hand the defence of his

eastern frontier against the slow but persistent pressure
of the Russians, Daun's effort to anticipate or keep up
with his rapid movements were almost ludicrously inadequate. While Frederick was learning at Zorndorf
(August 25, 1758) the stubborn value of the Russian
soldier, the Austrian commander contented himself with
slowly gathering his troops round Dresden, only to
withdraw on the return of the king from his hard-won
northern victory. There was still hope that some
success might attend the efforts of the Austrian generals
who were besieging the Silesian fortresses of Kosel and
Neisse. The hope at one time approached a certainty.
Frederick, eager to relieve these fortresses, slipped away
from Dresden and marched towards Silesia. Daun for
once showed himself capable of rapid movement, outmarched the king, and barred his road at Hochkirch.
In reckless contempt for the man who never seemed to
strike a blow, Frederick allowed himself to be surrounded,
and suffered what would to any other man have been a
crushing defeat (October 14, 1758). But quickly gathering his forces together, he again passed his sluggish
adversary and saved his Silesian fortresses. The hopes
of Daun had been very high after Hochkirch; but his
attack upon Dresden, though supported by the army of
the Empire, failed before the vigorous resistance offered
by General Schmettau, and again the return of the king
from his successful Silesian expedition drove him to
withdraw into Bohemia.

The attack on Olmütz had filled Vienna with con-
sternation. The empress was urged to retire from her
capital and seek a safer home in Gratz. But it was not at
a time of crisis such as this that any womanly weakness

was found in the empress. Feeling bitterly that she had
been ill served, and that a great mistake had been committed in denuding Moravia of troops, she yet absolutely
refused to move unless she saw the enemy before the
gates. The raising of the siege of Olmütz filled her
with fresh confidence in her commanders; her gratitude
to Daun and Laudon was extreme. As far as the political situation was concerned, she did not overrate the
value of this success. In the wavering councils of her
French allies, the grudging acquiescence in her policy
which she had secured was again breaking down before
continued disaster. Clermont, the new French commander, had given way in all directions before the forces
of Ferdinand of Brunswick; he had retired behind the
Weser and behind the Rhine. Even there he had been
assaulted. On June 23, just before the raising of the
siege of Olmütz, he had suffered a complete defeat at
Crefeld. During the whole of the spring, correspondence
had poured in from Paris, speaking of nothing but
despondency and desire for peace. Even Stahremberg
was beginning to lose hope. It was in vain that
Kaunitz plied him with despatches replete with encouraging arguments. "The character of the court
is such," the ambassador replied, "that no reliance
can be placed in it. Cabals, intrigues, and personal
interests deprive it of all stability." He was driven
to confess that there was no hope of real assistance
from France, and that as the prosecution of the war
without such assistance was impossible, there was
nothing left but to make peace. The news from
Olmütz for a while changed this despondency into
triumph, the complaints of Austrian idleness and want

of energy were silenced. Belleisle wrote to Kaunitz, expressing his earnest wish that Daun could be at once in Moravia and on the Rhine. Such expressions were no doubt cheering. Yet no real help came from France. Better generals, Contades and Soubise, were indeed appointed and more vigour was shown. But the skill of Ferdinand gave them full employment, and prevented them from producing any real effect upon the course of the war; even when their efforts were crowned with some success, he contrived to keep their armies apart and neutralise any advantages they had gained.

Throughout the campaign Maria Theresa took the keenest interest in the military operations and displayed an insight which is truly remarkable. Yet the same mistaken attempt, not wholly conscious, to manage the war from Vienna is apparent. Again and again she declared that she would lay no commands upon Daun, but leave him entirely free; yet she sent him despatch after despatch, discussing events with him both from a political and military point of view, and practically marking out the direction of his actions. Her keen eye at once saw the intention of Frederick when he left Silesia for the north; she understood and explained to her general the necessity of rapidly getting into touch with the Russians. She immediately recognised the futile character of his efforts to do so, and pointed out the opportunity during the king's absence of rapid and effective action in Saxony. Yet, as was almost inevitable, though she constantly spoke of the necessity of some great and striking success, she never ventured to give a direct order that the field-marshal should risk a battle. In fact one trait of her

character, fine in itself, was not without bad effect upon
a war thus managed with divided authority. Her confidence once given, her admiration once won, were of a
most enduring description, most difficult to be shaken.
As she had clung in her early years to her inefficient
ministers, as she had allowed her armies to be wasted
under the undecided command of her brother-in-law,
so now she put her trust in Daun, and did not suffer
the wearisome slowness of his proceedings and their
barrenness in great results to shake her confidence in
him. His triumph at Hochkirch seemed a justification
of her good opinion. She rained honours upon him.
Even when the strange ineffectual sequel of his Hochkirch
triumph was exciting the strongest public reprobation
she remained true to him. So sharp appeared the
public expression of disapproval that he was thinking
of resigning. She instructed Haugwitz under these
circumstances to write to him and to assure him that
"the empress with tears in her eyes had expressed
her heartfelt desire that Field-Marshal Daun might
continue to render to her and to the state the same
incalculable services as heretofore"; she looked upon
him "as her most precious and true house-treasure."
In this desire Kaunitz also participated. "I hold you,"
he wrote, "as the best soldier we can find; I cannot
therefore recommend any other commander for our
army, and am sure that as an honest man and a
good citizen you will not leave us in the lurch."
The empress did not confine herself to words. She
settled a handsome fortune upon him and his descendants, and accompanied her gift with the most graceful
and affectionate letter. Indeed her confidence in her

field-marshal never flagged. It was unshaken even
by his conduct in the campaign of 1759, when Frederick
himself confessed that the allies had nothing left to do
but to give him his *coup de grace*, and yet Daun in his
exasperating over-caution failed to deliver the blow,
and thus rendered resultless all the successes that had
been gained. The Prince of Hildburghausen, who had
withdrawn from the command of the Imperial army and
was living in retirement in Vienna, playing the part of
the candid critic, wrote to her strongly on the subject.
His letter is endorsed in her own hand, " If Daun had
had more efficient helpers he would no doubt have been
a greater man."

Though the campaign of 1758 had produced no great
results, it had not been disastrous to the allies; it had
been marked by at least one great victory, and the
course of French disaster had been checked. But enough
had not been done to cheer the failing heart of Bernis;
he continued to besiege the court of Vienna with suggestions of the necessity of peace. Kaunitz had even been
obliged to show some signs of sympathy, and to confine
himself to the entreaty that one campaign more might
be tried in hope that some striking success might
prevent the peace which seemed inevitable from being
of a humiliating character. The timid counsels of
Bernis had been faithfully delivered by Stainville
his representative at Vienna, and his arguments had
even been urged with warmth and impetuosity. But
Stainville's own opinion had not corresponded with
his instructions. He listened with favour to the more
courageous replies of Kaunitz, and wrote despatches
strongly advocating the maintenance of the new system

of alliances whatever the course of the war might be.
It was therefore no slight encouragement to the Austrian
court in its constant dread of the wavering policy of
Bernis, when a mark of distinguished royal favour,
which appeared to show that King Louis was still
firm in his friendship, was accorded to Stainville and
he was raised to the rank of Duke of Choiseul, and
summoned to Paris to take the portfolio of foreign
affairs. The change of ministry, however, proved less
satisfactory than had been anticipated. The vehement
and self-asserting character of the new minister formed
undoubtedly a marked contrast to the vacillation of his
predecessor. It proved to be far easier to carry on
negotiations with him ; at all events he knew his own
mind, and had a remarkably clear view of one side of
any question he approached. But, somewhat to the
surprise of Kaunitz, his view of the situation now
that he was minister was not exactly that which had
found expression in the late treaty, and which was
held by the Austrian court. Choiseul was too good
a Frenchman to suffer his country to be dragged deeper
into difficulties by its ally ; and he felt obliged, in the
responsible position which he now held, to confess that
Bernis had been right in declaring the actual impossibility of giving effect to the promises which had been
made. He therefore at once set to work, and successfully,
to arrange a new treaty. Not only were the subsidies
considerably lowered, but the terms of the Treaty of
Versailles so modified as to show very clearly the effect
produced by the unexpected resistance of Prussia. The
possibility of the reconquest of Silesia was indeed still
contemplated ; the two courts still pledged themselves

to secure if possible some indemnity beyond the mere
restitution of his estates to the Elector of Saxony;
their respective conquests were guaranteed, and certain
cessions secured to France if Maria Theresa should
succeed in winning any substantial accession of territory
from the Prussian king. But there was no longer any
mention of the great exchange, or of the establishment
of a French prince in the Low Countries, nor would
France in any way pledge itself to the restoration of the
lost provinces. The certainty of success had entirely
disappeared, and the former arrangements had become
merely conditional.

To induce the French court to agree to this treaty
it was necessary to offer something beyond mere hope.
Events having rendered the satisfaction of the French
king's desire to obtain the Low Countries for his son-
in-law highly improbable, another satisfaction of his
wishes with respect to his family was found. The
Austrian court consented to run the risk of breaking
off negotiations which had been entered into with the
King of Naples, for the marriage of his eldest daughter
with the Archduke Joseph. They suggested that the
archduke should be contracted to the Princess Isabella
of Parma, whose mother was Louis's favourite daughter.
By this means, if the mother could not obtain her
settlement in the Netherlands, her daughter had every
prospect of becoming the wife of the head of the
Hapsburg House and Empress. The ruffled feelings
of the Neapolitan court were soothed by the substitution of Maria Theresa's second son Charles for
his brother, and by the erection of Tuscany into a
quasi-independent appanage in his favour. Kaunitz,

though not usually troubled with modesty, was ashamed
to approach the King of Naples with the unvarnished
excuse of political necessity; he was forced to rest
the change of suitors on the determined preference
of Joseph himself.   It is characteristic of Maria
Theresa that she entirely objected to this finesse.   She
insisted that the marriage of Joseph should not be
treated as a matter of choice; as a well-brought-up son
she thought he could not insist on such a thing; it
should be regarded as a state necessity settled by the
Conference.   Neither could she approve of any portion
of her dominions being even partially severed from the
central government.   As usual, however, she allowed
Kaunitz and reasons of state to overrule her own conscientious objections.

The campaign of 1759, which proved to be in some
respects the most critical of the war, opened under
somewhat different conditions from those which had
preceded it.

The activity of the Prussian king had hitherto
spared the allies the difficulty of deciding upon the
plan of campaign.   They had been compelled to follow
the line marked out for them by their untiring opponent.   But the king's resources, which had already
proved inadequate for the decisive results he had
anticipated, were now much reduced, and the allies
had now the task of choosing for themselves the direction which the war should take.   It was no easy matter
to arrive at a decision.   The interests and desires
of France and Russia were by no means the same.   It
was natural that both of them should wish the action of
the Austrian generals to be such as to bring their forces

into immediate connection with their own operations.
To France also the fate of its old ally Saxony was a
matter of supreme importance. Thus in the plans
suggested by the court of Versailles, the chief efforts of
the Austrian armies were to be directed to the reconquest
of Saxony in close co-operation with the French armies
advancing from the Rhine. To Russia, on the other
hand, the presence of the main army in Silesia and the
Lausitz, in immediate co-operation with its own forces
advancing through Poland upon the Lower Oder, seemed
to promise far better results. It might have been
expected that so immediately after the signing of the
revised treaty, and the apparent renewal of the closest
amity with the French, their influence would have been
decisive; but Maria Theresa, to whom the decision
necessarily fell, gave full support to the Russian view.
The mere fact that it seemed to promise the reconquest
of Silesia, the real aim of all her hopes, might well have
induced her to assume this attitude; but it is plain
from her letters that she had other reasons. Her eyes
had become opened to the real weakness of the policy
of the Versailles Treaty; she had conceived a strong
disbelief in the probability of any real and whole-hearted
assistance from France. The new treaty had not removed her mistrust; she was convinced that if any
substantial advantage was to be won, it was to Russian
co-operation that she must look. The fact, which might
have been patent at first had she not been blinded by
hatred for England and Prussia, had gradually forced
itself on her, that whether her western ally was France
or England, the rivalry of those countries was too strong
to allow them to lose sight of their own particular

interests; whatever alliances they might form in Europe
were certain to be subsidiary to their own all-important
quarrel, and nothing could prevent the war, as at present
carried on, from being practically twofold.

The discussions required to arrive at any definite
plan of action, added to the natural slowness of the
Austrian commander, postponed till late in the year the
opening of the campaign.   The plan adopted gave to
the main Austrian army, under the immediate command
of Daun, the duty of operating in Silesia; while the
troops of the Empire, supported if possible by French
allies, were left to operate in Saxony.   When once in
motion, the field-marshal exhibited considerable skill.
Adopting his usual dilatory tactics, he retained Frederick
upon the borders of Silesia while he despatched an
important detachment under the command of Laudon
and Haddick, with instructions to join the Russian
troops advancing from Posen, and fall upon the rear of
the king.   The departure of this detachment was so
well arranged that its ultimate destination was not
known; but by degrees, as news was brought to
Frederick of the Russian advance, the danger of his
position became obvious.   At first, not willing to leave
Silesia uncovered, he trusted to his generals in Brandenburg, Dohna and Wedel, to deal with the Russians;
but after their unsuccessful battle at Züllichau (July 23,
1759), and after his discovery of the destination of the
Austrian detachment, it became of vital importance to
him to prevent, if possible, a junction which would give
an irresistible superiority to the armies advancing upon
his eastern frontier.   In hot haste he broke up his camp
at Schmöttseifen, and hurried off upon this errand.

But he found in Laudon an enemy whose rapidity and
decision almost equalled his own. His pursuit was
unavailing. Leaving Haddick behind him, Laudon
pressed on with 20,000 men, outmarched and evaded
the king, and when Frederick arrived at Frankfort on
the Oder, he found the junction already effected, and
the combined army of Russians and Austrians taking
position on the heights of Kunersdorf, on the farther
side of the river. It was necessary to bring them to
an engagement. He crossed the Oder a little below
Frankfort, marched in front of the Russian position,
and fell with all his forces upon their right or eastern
wing. His first assaults were successful; the enemy fell
back westward along the ridge, and everything promised
a complete victory. But the stubborn obstinacy of the
Russians, which is their great military virtue, enabled
them to delay his advance, and the approach of Laudon
with his fresh troops changed the fortune of the day.
The lost ground was regained, and the Prussian army to
all appearance irretrievably ruined (August 12, 1759).

So heavy was the blow, that Frederick seemed for the
moment crushed by it; he gave way to despair, made
arrangements for handing over the army to his brother
Henry, and even thought of putting an end to his life.
His position was, indeed, almost desperate. His own
dominions, his own capital seemed to lie open to the
advance of the victorious Russians; his brother had
been compelled to occupy the place which the king's
march northward had left empty in front of Daun's
army, and Saxony was almost denuded of troops. And
on that side the army of the Empire was now advancing
with little or no opposition; fortress after fortress fell

into its hands, and it crowned its achievements by the reconquest of Dresden. But the despair of Frederick was of short duration. In four days he had recovered all his habitual energy. The commandant of Dresden, had he but known it, might have saved the capital; reinforcements from the king were already in its immediate neighbourhood, and although foiled in their main object of saving the city, the Prussians were still able so far to regain what they had lost in Saxony, and so completely to establish their authority there, that Daun with his Silesian army was compelled to march to oppose them. It was, of course, a necessary part of the concerted scheme that the victorious Russians should be able to give full employment to the king himself. But in spite of the reiterated solicitations of Daun, they refused to act with vigour. The king was left free for the defence of Saxony, and when, by an extraordinary march, Prince Henry brought his troops up from Silesia and formed a junction with his brother, the fortunes of the campaign entirely changed. Unable as usual to take advantage of the superiority of his numbers, Daun found himself compelled to fall slowly backward towards Bohemia, and the campaign which had promised so well was only saved from a disgraceful termination by the overconfidence of the Prussians. Not content to allow Daun to retire unmolested, Frederick pushed forward a corps of 12,000 men under General Finck to take up a position at Maxen among the hills to the south of Dresden and harass the Austrian retreat. It was certain that so small a body could have no chance of success if Daun should prove courageous enough to attack it, and no doubt Finck should have used his judgment in the

matter. He appears to have misunderstood some ill-
considered words of the king, and, when both the field-
marshal himself and the army of the Empire closed
round him, he determined to hold his ground. The
event was inevitable. Surrounded by vastly superior
troops, after a brave resistance, he was obliged to capitu-
late with all that was left of his corps, and Dresden
with its neighbourhood remained in the hands of the
allies.

This small success, though it was treated by the
Austrians with all the honours of a great victory, could
scarcely be considered a satisfactory result of a campaign
in which Frederick might surely have been annihilated.
No doubt something may be said for Daun. The inactivity of the Russians thwarted his schemes ; but for
that inactivity he was himself largely to blame. The
extraordinary slowness which he had always exhibited
had excited much disgust in their minds ; they could not
persuade themselves to trust in any active co-operation
from their allies, or divest themselves of the notion
that the whole brunt of the fighting was thrown upon
them, when they saw that, while they had twice defeated
the redoubtable Prussian troops, Daun with the constant command of vastly superior forces had effected
nothing. No doubt also the victory which Ferdinand
of Brunswick had won over the French at Minden (Aug.
1, 1759) had contributed to the failure of the campaign,
but there can be little question that with the aid of the
Imperial troops, inferior though they were, no difficulty
should have been found in overwhelming the weakened
forces of the Prussian king.

Politically the affair of Maxen was of more import-

ance.   It again postponed the breaking up of the
alliance, and the conclusion of a peace to which
the French court was gradually making up its mind.
This was the more important, because during this
autumn signs were visible that the enemies of Austria
were also beginning to feel the uselessness of a pro-
longed war, and to entertain thoughts of peace.   The
kings of England and of Prussia had employed the good
offices of Prince Louis of Brunswick, the guardian of
the infant Stadtholder, to place in the hands of the
ambassadors of France, Austria, and Russia, at the
Hague, a joint declaration in favour of a general
congress.   There was much to recommend such a
step, and some prospect that the idea would meet
with general acceptance.   The events of the late
campaign had produced bitter recriminations between
the courts of Vienna and St. Petersburg.   France,
exhausted by its naval war, was already seeking the
intervention of Spain in behalf of a separate treaty.
The alliance seemed to be dissolving, and the best
hope of Austria for obtaining advantageous terms
might well be thought to rest upon a general European
settlement.   But as yet the statesmen of Vienna did
not take that view.   Small and indecisive though
their successes had been, they had yet been successes;
nor could they persuade themselves that the resources
of Prussia after its late heavy losses were sufficient to
continue the contest much longer.   They also knew
that Pitt had made it clearly understood that if a
congress were called he would not allow the two
branches of the war to be treated separately.   As the
arrangements would necessarily depend chiefly upon

M

the respective advantages gained in the war, Kaunitz
dreaded lest the Austrian successes, when they came
to be weighed in a general balance, should be absolutely
neutralised by the disasters France had encountered at
the hands of England. Nor could he be sure from the
language used by the French ministers that they would
not adopt the policy of Pitt, and use the successes of
Austria to obtain better terms for France. But though
determined, for the present at least, to reject the
congress, Kaunitz was afraid that the open assertion
of a policy leading to the indefinite continuation of the
war would shock the feeling of Europe. Without
therefore speaking plainly on the matter, he devoted
all his diplomatic ability to postponing the summoning
of the congress till the opening of a new campaign
should have afforded Austria one more chance at
least of securing a great success. But in fact his
diplomacy was somewhat wasted. He had no real
reason to expect that a congress would be called.
It seems certain that Choiseul in flirting with the
idea was merely attempting to play with Frederick,
while he was more earnestly engaged in the effort to
contract a separate peace with England ; and that the
Czarina had no intention of allowing the angry feelings
roused by the inefficiency of the military co-operation
of Austria to interfere with her implacable determination to humble Prussia, or with the realisation of the very
advantageous peace which she pictured to herself as
possible.

But if the congress was not to be, if Kaunitz's efforts
at postponing it were but waste labour, the delicate
work of maintaining the alliance he had created still

taxed his powers to the utmost. To show her determination to be true to her engagements, the Czarina
demanded a new treaty. Well aware that her co-
operation in the field was absolutely necessary to
Austria, she determined to sell it at a high price.
The treaty which had been contracted at the beginning
of the war, giving the kingdom of East Prussia to
an Austrian prince, was thrown aside; and she now
insisted that, as her troops were in permanent occupation of that province, it should be secured to her
in case of peace. One of the clauses in the revised
French treaty demanded that neither of the contracting
parties should enter into engagements with other
countries without the full knowledge of its confederate.
But it was impossible to believe that France would
approve of a large acquisition on the part of Russia,
which threatened its cherished influence on the north-
east of Europe; and it was plain that Maria Theresa
had entered into the treaty with Russia without the
knowledge of France. With great misgivings, Kaunitz
yielded to the scruples of his mistress, and instructed
his ambassador to inform the French court, and to make
the best of what had been done. The peculiarity of
Choiseul's disposition saved Kaunitz from a very
awkward complication. It was a marked characteristic
of the French minister that he became feverishly intent
upon the immediate object before him to the exclusion
of all others. Deeply engaged at the moment in his
negotiations with England, he received the information
of the Russian treaty with perfect indifference, and the
difficulty passed over.

The Austrian chancellor, at the beginning of the year

1760, might well pride himself on his diplomatic success. He had steered skilfully through the dangers which had threatened to wreck the great alliance. The congress, which might easily have proved fatal to it, was no more heard of; and Austria was ready to enter upon a new campaign, side by side with its two great allies, bound to it by freshly-made treaties.

CHAPTER VIII

THE SEVEN YEARS' WAR (*continued*)

1760-1763

THE lengthened and somewhat pedantic discussions, which during the winter had occupied the attention of the generals and the members of the ministry of war, had left the settlement of the plan to be adopted in the hands of Maria Theresa herself.

During the late campaign, two commanders, Lacy and Laudon, had raised themselves above the general level. Both of them were comparatively young in the service, but very different in their temperaments and abilities. Lacy, a man of good birth and education, was regarded as a master of strategy, and found in Daun an ardent supporter. He had become the field-marshal's right hand man, to whom could be entrusted the execution of any plans requiring rapidity and daring, while his advice was scientific and cautious enough to suit Daun's own peculiar genius. Laudon, less distinguished by birth, was little more than a soldier of fortune, a master of tactics, and a leader fitted to inspire the troops with that audacity and readiness to strike which was so much wanted in the Austrian army. Kaunitz, who mingled in all warlike discussions, and groaned under the lifeless system of Daun which was constantly threatening the dissolution of his favourite political plans, was the staunch supporter of Laudon. A considerable rivalry had arisen between these two leaders ; while the jealousy with which they were regarded by the older generals, on account of their comparatively junior position in the army list, rendered it difficult to employ either of them in chief commands. The discussions had centred mainly upon the plans which they had suggested. Lacy, who seems to have been much struck with the inferiority of his own soldiers in actual battle, and with the lukewarmness of the Russian co-operation, urged a defensive war in Saxony, until the superiority of numbers and the unavoidable dissemination of the smaller army of the Prussians should give an opportunity for striking some effectual blow. Laudon was for the immediate adoption of vigorous offensive action in Silesia, with the co-operation of a strong Russian corps which should be placed directly under the command of an Austrian general.

The natural impulses of the empress led her to favour the view of Laudon. She could not hide from herself that, in spite of the success at Maxen, Daun's want of enterprise had wasted the great opportunity of the last campaign. But, with her usual great-hearted confidence in her old friends, she could not dream of removing him from the command, and finally decided upon a sort of compromise by which the field-marshal was left to operate with the grand army in Saxony, while Laudon was entrusted with a second force in

Silesia, where he was permitted, practically unrestrained, to carry out his own vigorous plans.

Laudon had at first to act alone, for no representations could induce the Russians to trust the ally who
seemed continually to use them as a cat's-paw, or could
remove their belief in the inefficiency of Austrian
generalship. But, though thus single-handed, Laudon
did not disappoint the expectations formed of him.
The destruction of a Prussian army corps under
General Fouquet at Landshut, the brilliant escalade
of the fortress of Glatz which covered the entrance
into Silesia, and a rapid advance upon Breslau, where
he hoped to be joined by a corps of Russians who had
moved readily enough when they saw the Austrians
bestirring themselves, marked the opening of his
campaign. But there his good fortune ceased; a
sudden march of Prince Henry snatched Breslau from
his grasp. Yet his advance had seemed so threatening
that the king had felt it necessary to come himself with
his Saxon army to the rescue of Silesia. Closely
followed by the armies of Daun and Lacy, and unable
to form a junction with his brother, the king appeared
to be marching to inevitable ruin. But, as usual, the
presence of the field-marshal threw a fatal spell over
the activity of the Austrian army. It was in vain
that the empress urged upon him the necessity of
making some final and decisive use of his superior
forces; her impatient and frequent despatches seemed
of no avail to drive him from his dilatory tactics.

At length, on August 15, when the armies lay
in the neighbourhood of Liegnitz, the field-marshal
made up his mind to attempt a threefold assault. To

Laudon was entrusted the task of occupying a range of heights stretching to the north and east of Liegnitz, thus cutting off the king's communication with his brother. Leaving his camp in the dead of night with the fires still burning, he proceeded to execute the movement. To his surprise he found the king with the whole Prussian army already occupying the heights. Though he persisted in his attack, and displayed both skill and tenacity in the assault, the strength of the position and the superiority of the king's forces rendered his defeat inevitable.

That the forces of Daun and Lacy lay comparatively idle, within reach of the battle, and did nothing to save their hard-pressed comrade was regarded as extraordinary at the time, and has never been fully explained. Their conduct excited great astonishment and anger. Bitter recriminations followed, and the public voice did not scruple to attribute base motives of jealousy both to Daun himself and to Lacy. In the midst of the general outcry, the position of Maria Theresa was very difficult. Like the chancellor, in her heart she fully sympathised with Laudon; but it was impossible for her to attribute to a man of Daun's character so unworthy a motive as personal jealousy. She met the difficulty with great tact. While sending to the field-marshal expressions of her unshaken confidence, to Laudon she wrote encouraging and soothing letters assuring him of the continuance of her favour. But she practically made Laudon's position henceforward independent, requesting him only as a matter of form to show his plans to the commander-in-chief.

As far as Silesia was concerned, the campaign had

been ruined by the battle of Liegnitz. The Russians
at once fell back towards their main body, and the
Austrians had to be satisfied with holding Glatz. But
Saxony still afforded a possible field for active operations.
For several weeks Daun and Frederick lay opposite each
other in the Silesian mountains, and it seemed as though
the king's activity would gradually oblige the field-
marshal to retire and close an inglorious campaign. It
was now Lacy's turn to give a direction to the war. With
a corps of 15,000 men detached from Daun's army, he
moved straight upon Berlin, towards which the Russian
troops were slowly rolling on through Brandenburg.
The raid, for it was not much more, was successful; the
Russians occupied the city, and were there joined by
Lacy. The blow to the prestige of Frederick was
heavy; and though the occupation of the capital had
in itself but little effect upon the war, it seemed to open
a vista of great future successes. For the king was at
once obliged to hurry northward; and, freed by his
departure from the pressure which was bidding fair to
ruin him, Daun was able to move into Saxony. Though
nothing more could be effected in Silesia, there was still
an opportunity for restoring the King of Poland to his
electoral dominions. The country was overrun, fortress
after fortress fell, and the field-marshal at length established himself at Torgau, on the left bank of the
Elbe, considerably north of Dresden. His position was
regarded as impregnable. But again the prospect of a
great success disappeared. Frederick would not surrender Saxony without a struggle, and decided to attack
Daun, despite all difficulties. The battle (Nov. 3, 1760)
was one of the bloodiest in the war, and full of striking

incidents. The Austrians occupied a ridge running westward at right angles to the river. In the judgment of
the king, a double assault both on the north and on the
south side of the ridge was necessary to dislodge them.
A twofold assault, when there is no complete communication between the parts, must always be a critical
movement. It was especially so in this instance. For
the troops entrusted with the assault on the north,
under the king's personal command, were obliged to
sweep round the western end of the ridge over the ill-
defined roads of a difficult woodland. Frederick found
himself suddenly in face of the enemy with a part only
of his troops, and at the same time was led to believe
by the sound of artillery that the attack upon the south,
which had been entrusted to Ziethen, was already in
progress. In fact Ziethen had changed his appointed
line of march and been drawn into a useless action, in
no way affecting the position which was to have been
assaulted. In ignorance of the erroneous line taken by
his lieutenant, the king, anxious that the two assaults
should be simultaneous, determined to begin the battle
with such troops as he had. His assault upon the
Austrian position, three times renewed with great vigour
and with heavy loss, was finally unsuccessful, and he
withdrew thinking that the day was lost. Daun had
been wounded and had left the field, but when informed
of Frederick's withdrawal he sent off immediate news
to Vienna of the victory he had won. Scarcely had the
messenger started, when, as night closed in, the battle
suddenly blazed up again. Ziethen had at last got into
his right direction, and was vehemently assaulting from
the south. Frederick's forces, who were bivouacking

close to the battlefield, sprang again to arms; a hill,
which was the key of the whole position, was captured
by the combined assault, and the Austrians were swept
back towards the Elbe.   Daun and his generals managed
to cross the river without a complete rout, but the
battlefield was entirely in the hands of the Prussians.

The news of the sad change of fortune was at once
despatched to Vienna, but the messenger was unable
to overtake the news of the victory.   Two miles outside
the city, Daun's first courier halted, and sent on his good
news to the empress.   Full of joy, she ordered, according to the fashion of the time, that the news should be
brought into the city in a triumphal procession of
couriers and trumpeters.   It is easy to conceive the
terrible reaction which fell on court and people when
the belated messenger arrived a few hours later, with
the true account of the conclusion of the day.   Some
comfort was found in the equality of loss suffered by
the two armies, and in the masterly retreat effected by
Lacy and his corps on the left bank of the river.   But
the real completeness of the blow needed no proof when
the field-marshal was seen withdrawing his army from
Saxony, and falling back into winter quarters in his old
position near Dresden, glad enough to retain even that
city.   Another indecisive campaign had indeed exhausted
both parties, but had brought no nearer the king's
humiliation, which was the object of the war.

Exhaustion, however, was beginning to do what
fighting had failed to do.   More especially was its effect
felt in France.   Choiseul, a man of moods, easily
depressed and easily exhilarated, changed his language
as the fortunes of war swayed to and fro; but on the

whole he was beginning to feel sure that, for France at
least, peace was a matter of necessity. He was not a
comfortable minister to work with. It required all the
cold and self-contained determination of Kaunitz to
meet unmoved his hot and cold fits, and to maintain
the friendship constantly placed in jeopardy by the
unchecked vehemence of his language. Upon Daun
especially, and his management of the war, Choiseul
opened all the vials of his wrath. Had the empress
been left to herself, this assault upon a man whom, in
spite of his want of success, she still regarded with
gratitude and confidence, would have roused her to
angry recriminations. But her minister was determined
to prevent any breach in the alliance which had been his
great work. By careful reiteration of its advantages, he
persuaded her that it must be preserved; he explained
away her occasional outbursts of hot speech to the
French ambassador; and with extreme tact, refraining
from urging the treaty claims of Austria, professed no
objection to an honourable peace.

In fact Kaunitz was himself beginning to think that
peace would soon be necessary, and that it might not
be such a peace as he had desired. With careful, almost
pedantic accuracy, he formulated no less than five forms
of peace which he considered possible. The best would
be if the empress could win Silesia and Glatz, without
giving any equivalent to France, while at the same time
her allies were properly indemnified at the expense of
Prussia, whose power would thus be largely reduced.
It would still be a good peace if she had to pay some
equivalent to France. It would be a moderate peace,
if she could secure for herself a part of Silesia, even if

the reduction of Prussia by indemnifications given to
her allies was found impossible. If she succeeded in
adding only some small scrap of territory to her
dominions, the peace would be barely satisfactory.
But the worst event of all would be the re-establish-
ment of the *status quo*. Both the first and second of
these alternatives seemed already beyond her grasp.
Much care would be necessary to secure even the peace
on moderate terms; for the negotiations of the previous
year had made it plain that there was immediate danger
of a separate treaty between France and England.
Such a peace he considered could be won only by the
constant co-operation of the allies, by success in the
war which must therefore be continued, and by some
form of general congress. Only by means of some such
assembly could the demands of friends and foes be alike
arrived at, and the general give and take, on which their
satisfaction must rest, be secured. But if there were
such a congress, he was not inclined to restrict his
demands to the acquisition of Silesia and Glatz. In
the general arrangement he thought that Anspach and
Baireuth, which seemed on the point of falling to
Frederick, might be handled so as to form a separate
and second possession of the Brandenburg House; while
in the threatened extinction of the male heirs of the
Bavarian Elector he saw a possibility of raising Imperial
or Austrian claims which should secure a portion of
the Electorate to Austria. Firmly rejecting, therefore,
Choiseul's suggestion that England and France should
appear as the chief negotiators, he urged that a general
congress should be summoned. His proposal was accepted; even the place of meeting, Augsburg, was settled.

Meanwhile it was clear that, as the assembling of
any such congress would take a considerable time, the
war must continue for at least one campaign more.
There was again some difficulty in deciding to whom
the chief command should be entrusted. With her
wonted magnanimity the empress had gone out of her
way to receive the defeated and wounded field-marshal
on his return from Torgau, and had heaped marks of her
favour on him ; but his credit had been seriously affected
by his want of success. The public voice, with the full
sympathy of Kaunitz, called persistently for Laudon.
The partisans of Lacy were not idle. But the extreme
dislike of their seniors to serve under either of these
younger generals rendered the reappointment of Daun
necessary. His superiority, however, was chiefly in
name ; the part he was to play was secondary ; while
keeping the king employed in Saxony, he was instructed
to support with all the troops he could spare the more
active warfare in Silesia, where Laudon was placed in
command. Frederick soon understood that Daun's
position was merely defensive, and hurried away to
encounter his more serious opponent in Silesia. Laudon's
movements were at first a disappointment to his supporters ; the decisive battles they had expected did not
take place ; he contented himself with manœuvring to
effect a junction with the Russian army under Marshal
Butterlin, who had agreed to march through Posen to
his assistance. Even with the enormous preponderance
of strength which was in his hands after the junction
was successfully effected, he was unable to drive the
king from the entrenched camp he had established at
Bunzelwitz. The patience of the Russians became

exhausted; their main army marched away northward, leaving only a corps under Czernichef to co-operate with Laudon. The campaign seemed ending in failure, when a brilliant deed of arms rescued it from that fate. Weary of enforced inactivity, the Prussian king left his stronghold and moved eastward, expecting that as usual the Austrian troops would follow his line of march. To his dismay Laudon let him go, and suddenly falling upon the great fortress and magazine of Schweidnitz captured it by escalade. It was indeed more than a brilliant deed of arms, it carried with it a political triumph. When all men believed that a congress was at hand, and that the terms of peace would depend largely upon the territory at the moment in possession of the belligerents, the acquisition of so considerable a portion of Silesia was a matter of the greatest importance. As such it was recognised not only in Vienna, but by Frederick. Scarcely even after the fatal field of Kunersdorf had his fortunes fallen so low.

But her success came too late for Maria Theresa. The lengthened war had brought her to the end of her resources; she was compelled, in spite of the protests of her generals, to make a substantial reduction in her army. In fact since the battle of Torgau the exhaustion of all the belligerents was so great that peace had become a matter of necessity. The Austrian court believed that the congress, which was actually appointed to meet in July, would sanction a peace on the basis of the "Uti possidetis." Such a peace would be far from disastrous to them. Frederick would have to resign Glatz, Schweidnitz, and part of Silesia, the whole of the kingdom of Prussia still occupied by the Russians, a part of

Pomerania, the duchy of Cleves, and the county of Mark.

That the congress never came into existence is due to the changeful and impulsive character of Choiseul, and to the irritation that he felt at his entanglement with Austria. In fact it may well be doubted whether he was ever in earnest in his acceptance of the idea. Peace was indeed as necessary for him as for any other of the belligerents; but the peace he required was with England and not with Prussia. He had been so successful in his overtures to the English Government that negotiators had been sent both to London and to Paris. In London not much advance had been made ; the cold attitude assumed by Pitt had proved an insurmountable obstacle. But in Paris, the English agent, John Stanley, had succeeded with much shrewdness and ability in so ingratiating himself with Choiseul that the terms of a treaty were actually formulated. With the attainment of his object thus close at hand, Choiseul found himself brought to a stop by the Versailles treaties of 1756. Stahremberg interposed, and pointed out that no fresh treaty could be contracted without the consent of the allies. The result of the Austrian interference was a vehement diplomatic contest between the two courts. The hot assertions of Choiseul and his violent struggles to break through the net in which he was entangled were constantly encountered by the passionless legalities of Kaunitz. There is no doubt that as far as treaty obligation went, the Austrian minister was upon safe ground. Choiseul was certainly seeking to use territory conquered by the allies for the purpose of effecting a favourable exchange with England,

in entire disregard of the duty which the treaties laid
upon him of finding compensation for the disinherited
Elector of Saxony. He had also certainly attempted to
effect a treaty without the leave of his Austrian ally.
But, as he pointed out, in any wider view his conduct
was strictly justifiable. It was, he said, ridiculous, and
could never have been intended, that Austria should
have a veto upon the arrangements between France and
England on questions peculiar to those two countries,
and which were in no way involved in the Prussian
war; such a stipulation would have placed all the
relations between France and England at the mercy of
the Austrian court. So reasonable was this contention,
that Kaunitz, afraid lest France should break loose, and
that all the advantages of his great treaties should slip
from him, instructed Stahremberg that it was not
advisable to overstrain the letter of the treaties. He
even expressed his willingness to withdraw his opposition to a separate peace upon certain conditions.
The clause of the old treaties requiring perfect confidence between the allies must be kept in sight, and
the consent of Russia must be obtained; it must also
be a separate peace in fact as well as in name; the
relations between Austria and Prussia must be entirely
excluded from it, and left for discussion at the congress;
and it must be expressly stated that neither France nor
England should henceforward give any assistance, direct
or indirect, to their allies. With this concession Choiseul
was satisfied, and the suggestions of Kaunitz were in-
corporated in the formàl propositions which at Pitt's
pressing instance were now laid before him.

But the peace was not yet to be. Choiseul's inventive

N

mind was already contemplating the great Bourbon
compact, which he regarded as the crowning triumph of
his ministry. He hoped to lay additional stress upon
England by incorporating certain Spanish grievances with
the French terms. Pitt indignantly and haughtily rejected what he stigmatised as the impertinent interference of the Spanish king. Thus repulsed, Choiseul
threw himself with his usual one-sided activity into
the completion of his arrangements with Spain, and,
supported by his new ally, cheerfully accepted the renewal of hostilities.

The sudden revival of warlike energy in the French
minister came as a shock to Kaunitz; for although he had
persistently thrown obstacles in the way of a separate
treaty, he was at heart anxious for the conclusion of
peace. Already the evident approach of the Czarina's
death was causing him grave misgivings; he was only
too well aware that the change of sovereigns in Russia
would rob him of his most powerful ally. The long-
dreaded event took place on January 6, 1762. The
old Czarina, Elizabeth, the implacable foe of Prussia,
passed away, and was succeeded by Frederick's enthusiastic admirer, the Grand Duke Peter. The effect was
instantaneous. In spite of profuse offers in the way of
subsidies, and of the most eager diplomatic representations, Austria saw its great alliance melting away. The
liberation of all the Prussian prisoners by Peter was
followed by a declaration in favour of peace, based upon
the complete restoration of conquered territories. The
peace was signed in May, the province of East Prussia
was restored, and the army in Silesia withdrawn.
Sweden speedily followed in the wake of its great neigh-

bour; and Frederick was thus freed from all disquietude
on his northern and eastern frontiers.

Events which had taken place in England seemed at
first likely to afford a compensation to the Austrians for
the loss of their Russian ally. The accession of George
III. was followed by a change of ministry which drove
Pitt from office, and the Prussian king could no longer
look to England, his only important ally, for assistance.
But in the sequel the change proved as disadvantageous
to Austria as to Prussia. An inefficient successor to
the great minister had been found in Bute, who was determined at all hazards to produce peace. The desertion
of his ally did not seem to him too high a price to pay.
While he opened negotiations with Austria, suggesting
the restoration of the old system of alliances and a united
effort to drive the Bourbons out of Italy, he approached
the Czar, suggesting that for the sake of peace Prussia
must be compelled to surrender a considerable portion
of Silesia. These overtures met the reception they
deserved. Kaunitz regarded them as a mere trap to
separate him from his French ally, and returned a
haughty refusal; Peter fell into a violent rage, and at
once pushed on his efforts in favour of Frederick. It
remained for Bute to adopt the plan of a separate
peace with France. In the pursuit of this object he was
more successful. He found Choiseul quite ready to fall
in with his views. Now that he was certain that peace
with England was easily within his reach, Choiseul acted
with perfect fairness, opened his projects to his allies and
consulted their opinions. Kaunitz still clung to the
view that a congress was desirable, but his hopes, as the
war went on, grew feebler and feebler; he confessed

that all prospect of weakening the Prussian power had
disappeared, and that he would be satisfied if the honour
of Austria could be saved by the acquisition of any
respectable territory such as Glatz, or some alteration
in the reversion of Anspach and Baireuth, which would
prevent those provinces from falling into the hands of
the reigning Prussian sovereign. The rumour that the
whole Russian army was marching to assist Frederick
made him withdraw even these moderate suggestions.
He threw up all hope of a congress, gave full leave that
Choiseul should contract a separate peace with England,
and even accepted the idea that the best solution of the
weary war was to treat it, as in fact it had always been,
as a twofold war, and to conclude the questions at issue
by two entirely different treaties

The rapid lowering of Austrian pretensions was
chiefly due to the unfavourable course of the war.
Czernichef's corps had not only been withdrawn from
co-operation with the Austrian army, but had taken
service under Frederick. Daun had been defeated at
Burkersdorf, and before the year was over Schweidnitz
had been recaptured. For a short time a sudden revival
of hope cheered the hearts of the statesmen in Vienna.
Peter of Russia had only been six months on the throne
when a revolution occurred which seemed likely to
produce as complete a change in the foreign politics of
the country as had been caused by his accession. He
was driven from his throne, which was at once occupied
by his wife Catherine; and almost immediately afterwards he was cruelly assassinated. It could not be
expected that the new Czarina, a partner in her
husband's dethronement, and in some ways the leader

of the discontent which had caused it, would pursue his
policy. In fact she began her reign by declaring her
endless animosity to the Prussian king. But all
probability of her returning to the hostile policy which
Elizabeth had always adopted towards Prussia speedily
disappeared. Her views, not confined to petty or
personal hatreds, embraced great policies both in the
South and in Poland. She at once recognised that for
her purposes it was better to have Frederick for a friend
than an enemy. Although, therefore, the troops which
Peter had sent to his aid were withdrawn, no hostile
step was taken against him, nor was the kingdom of
Prussia reoccupied; Austria found itself left single-
handed to deal with its formidable adversary.

When the great English minister, whose steadfast
adherence to his allies and rejection of external interference had stood in the way of previous negotiations, was
removed, no further obstacle was found to the immediate
conclusion of the preliminaries of an agreement between
England, France, and Spain. In face of the events which
had taken place in Russia, and the hopelessness of military
success, the empress could no longer refuse to give
her assent to the conclusion of the war by means of
two separate treaties. Every one whose opinion was
of importance in Vienna was now eager for peace. As
the news of little delays and hitches in the negotiations
were brought to Maria Theresa she never failed to
express her feeling of the necessity, not only of peace,
but of speedy peace. "So dark is the outlook," she wrote
in October 1762, "that we must either have immediate
peace, or none." The field-marshal was of the same
opinion. "If these preliminaries come to nothing," he

writes, "I do not see how your Majesty is to carry on the war, or how the army can hold its positions in the winter"; and then follows a disheartening description of sick and wearied troops and of thoroughly depressed officers. Kaunitz was equally convinced of the necessity. Even the emperor and Joseph, who seem to have been the last on whom the necessity forced itself, now withdrew their opposition. "Take your opportunity," writes the empress to Kaunitz, "while the emperor's views are favourable; they may easily change. At all events, at this moment both he and my son wish to bring matters to a conclusion."

The Austrian ambassador had therefore no duties with respect to the preliminaries of Fontainebleau, except to see that the interests of his country, which were inevitably intermixed with those of France, should suffer as little injury as possible. Stahremberg performed this duty well, and fought hard to secure the full payment of the arrears of subsidy which in the exhaustion of the Austrian treasury was a matter of great importance. He insisted also that Austrian troops should occupy those districts which, in accordance with the treaty, were to be evacuated. Louis and his ministers, the two Choiseuls, acted fairly enough to their ally. The king honestly declared that, whatever happened, the empress must be satisfied; and, on the eve of the signing of the preliminaries, a convention was made by which these two points were secured. But with regard to the cession of the conquered territory it was found impossible to fulfil the French promises, for no Austrian troops could be spared to garrison the vacated fortresses; nor was the matter of much importance, for all men

knew that the second separate treaty must be contracted
before many months were over.

With exhausted finances and a dispirited army, without allies, and with no advantage from long years of war
except the little conquest of Glatz, Maria Theresa
earnestly desired peace. But her spirit was not yet so
broken that she could seek it as a suppliant from her
victorious enemy. The intervention of some third
peacemaker was required. As under existing circumstances neither England, France, nor Russia was either
fitted or inclined to play the part of mediator, advantage
was taken of the miserable plight of the Saxon Elector
to throw a veil of dignity, which Kaunitz confessed to
be all he could now hope for, over what was in fact an
unconditional surrender. The Polish king, driven from
his electoral dominions and forced to see his subjects
suffering the extremest rigours of the war, was clamorous
for peace. As though unable to refuse the request of her
suffering ally, the empress authorised Augustus to discover the feelings of the Prussian king. The suggestion
of a peace found favour with Frederick, and negotiations
were at once begun. Collenbach was despatched, as a
spécial envoy, to meet the Prussian minister Herzberg,
with instructions not only to discuss but to complete an
immediate and definitive peace. Kaunitz still hoped
that in the general settlement some political advantages
might be secured. Anspach and Baireuth might be
saved from falling into the immediate possession of the
Prussian crown ; the arrangements he had made in Italy
might be accepted ; Hungary guaranteed against the
Turks ; nay, perhaps means might be found for retaining
the county of Glatz. But it is difficult to believe that

he cherished any real hope of carrying even these points.
In the face of the continued suffering ruthlessly imposed
upon Saxony, and of the avowed incapacity of Austria
to carry on the war, he could scarcely have expected
that his diplomacy would have effected much against
the firmness of Frederick. In every matter of importance
he was worsted; and after some months of fruitless
discussion the Vienna court was glad to ratify the
Treaty of Hubertsburg (February 15, 1763) upon the
basis of the Berlin Treaty of 1745. Glatz was not retained, the succession of Anspach and Baireuth was left
unaltered, the reciprocal guarantees were not extended
to Hungary; nothing was gained except the promise
of the Prussian vote for Joseph at the election of the
King of the Romans, and the recognition of the arrangements already made for the succession of Modena.

The futile and resultless expenditure of blood and
treasure, the years of useless suffering which had attended
her efforts to re-win Silesia, made a deep and lasting
impression upon the empress. From this time onward,
what she most dreaded was war. Her confidence in
Kaunitz, however, was not in the least shaken, and she
still regarded with persistent complacency the European
system which he had established. Yet it had produced
nothing but disaster. Though the long war had left
her with undiminished territory, it had certainly done
much to diminish her political prestige. With the aid
of powerful allies, with an apparently overwhelming
superiority of resources, she had been unable to gain
any advantage over a rival whom she still considered as
an upstart prince. It is at first difficult to understand
the tenacity with which she clung to her minister and to

his plans. She could not have failed to see that the
course on which she had embarked at his instigation had
led to misfortune. The political influence of Austria
had been seriously compromised. Both the main
object of the war and the collateral aims which had
arisen during its course had alike failed of realisation.
She stood without an ally. Her voice had not been
heard in the settlement of the great war between
England and France. No great nation sought her
friendship. It was in vain to pretend, as was pretended,
that she had reason to be satisfied with the Treaty of
Hubertsburg, or to try to hide the patent fact that her
position there was that of a suppliant. On the other
hand, her rival, far from suffering the humiliation, to
secure which Europe had been turned upside down, had
emerged from the long war, exhausted indeed and with
shattered resources, but in the position of a successful
first-rate Power.

It is in the character and talents of the empress
herself, and of her minister, that any explanation can be
found. Again and again in the time of crisis Maria
Theresa had proved that she was the most faithful
of friends. No failure, no mistake seemed able to
overshadow her admiration if once excited. Her confidence once given, was given wholly and never withdrawn. On his side, Kaunitz was exceptionally fitted
for the position which he occupied as the adviser and
the support of the high-spirited woman. The liveliness
of his imagination enabled him to understand the
views of his political opponents, and even to sympathise
with them. His large experience and acquaintance with
the world, joined to his somewhat cynical sharpness of

sight, enabled him to fathom the weaknesses of those
with whom he came in contact. Unscrupulous himself,
his ingenuity supplied him easily with plausible arguments to override the conscientious difficulties of his
mistress. His vast industry, the proofs of which are
shown in the mass of state papers and correspondence
which he left, led him to examine and set out with a
perspicuity almost pedantic the arguments for and
against the line of conduct that he submitted to her
judgment. But before all, the cause of her unflagging
confidence is to be found in his unquestionable and
unswerving devotion to her interests. Conceited and
eccentric as he was, he merged his own glory in the glory
of the empress, and subjected to his tenacious will every
sign of opposition, however high the quarter from which
it emanated. It was impossible for her to find a more
devoted or able assistant in realising that view of the
pre-eminence of the head of the state, which she had
conceived almost from the beginning of her reign, or in
giving effect to the duties implied by such a position.

The close friendship between the empress and her
chancellor was the more remarkable because in many
respects his personal characteristics seemed but little
fitted to attract such a woman as Maria Theresa. Proud
of his good looks, he gave himself all the airs of a
finished dandy, pluming himself on the delicacy of his
complexion and the elegance of his clothes. His con-
ceit was overweening. He was as proud of his skill as
a horseman as of his ability as a statesman, and delighted to exhibit himself in his riding school. He
early persuaded himself that he was a confirmed invalid,
and allowed himself all the liberties of a valetudinarian.

In his later life he treated both the empress and her
son with a freedom which in any other man would have
been resented as rudeness. His comfort had to be considered before that of his mistress. Her health required
her to sit at all times with open windows; when the
chancellor could be prevailed upon to call on her, which
was not always easy, his first step was to have them
closed. When her son became emperor, the chancellor
would often for days together carry on his communications
by writing; or if a personal interview was absolutely
necessary, it was the emperor who had to go and call
on the minister. But in her full reliance on the real
qualities which lay behind this strange affectation
Maria Theresa seems to have entirely forgotten the little
impertinences of her friend, and to have poured out
her heart to him in the fullest and most serious confidence.

CHAPTER IX

DOMESTIC AFFAIRS

1758-1765

THE years during which the war lasted had been full of gloom at the Vienna court. The change was a striking one; for in earlier times it had been full of gaiety and amusement. The young empress queen was formed by nature to take the lead in glad social life. Contemporaries tell us of her beauty, the lively brilliancy of her blue eyes, her lofty and intellectual forehead, her rich light hair, the delicate contour of her face, the beautiful lines of her neck, arms, and hands, and the lissom grace of her movements. No doubt it is easier for crowned heads to be beautiful than for ordinary subjects; but even making allowance for courtly admiration, it is certain that Maria Theresa was a woman of remarkably prepossessing appearance. Even as she grew older, after care, disaster, and illness had destroyed her bright complexion and added lines of firmness to her full lips, she is represented in all her pictures as a woman fair to look upon, gifted with an openness and strength which seem to invite or indeed to command trust and love.

She was of more than middle height, and glowing with good health. She delighted in exercise, and was so constant and fearless a horsewoman, that the formal interference of her ministers was thought necessary, to prevent her from injuring her health. Such a gifted girl, for she was but twenty-four when her reign began, had naturally thrown herself fully into the gaiety of the court, which showed itself, as the seasons changed, in balls and fêtes, sledging parties and tilting matches.

Very different was the aspect the court assumed in this period of serious and determined struggle. The empress could now endure no great public entertainments or balls; the card-table was interdicted, even the court dinner-parties were diminished. The financial pressure was very stringent; as early as 1758 the empress pawned her jewels; in 1760 a patriotic subscription was raised, and the officials sent their plate to be minted. Only now and then, when the news of the somewhat scanty victories was brought, and the officer who carried the despatches made his triumphant entry into the city, was the gloom lightened, and gaiety for a while re-established. Even then, it was less to gaiety than to religion that the empress turned to express her joy. The court life of the time was indeed coloured by the fervour of her religion. She was never weary of seeking the help of heaven in the war by public prayers, long religious services, and rigorous national fasts.

But if it was a time of social depression, it was also a time during which the machinery of the State underwent a rude trial. The reforms of Haugwitz had not proved thoroughly satisfactory. The keynote of those

reforms had been the formation of the centralised State;
they had at once and for ever broken the power of the
provincial Estates. But the change by which a federative
country, which in respect to the power and influence
of the nobles recalls a medieval or feudal aristocracy, was
metamorphosed into a well-organised despotism was not
one to be quickly carried out, especially when, as in
the present case, the head of the State was in all
her tastes essentially aristocratic. Maria Theresa
never for a moment questioned the hereditary claims
of her great nobles to consideration and employment; she never ceased to live on terms of close
friendship with them. She undoubtedly felt that she
belonged to a royal caste, and in all the matrimonial
arrangements which she made for her children she confined herself strictly within the limits of the reigning
Houses; but none the less did she admit to her close
personal friendship members of the higher nobility.
She sympathised in their family troubles and joys,
wrote to them in terms of affectionate intimacy, and
lavished favours on them with a hand almost too liberal,
considering the condition of her finances. Thus, the
relentless establishment of a strict administrative system,
where ability and service should be the sole ground for
employment or advance, was quite outside her conception
of the State. As a natural consequence the efforts
made to establish unification of government, apart from
the one great point of its emancipation from the influence of the provincial Estates, were of a tentative and
incomplete character.

In the opinion of some of the older and more con-
servative ministers, nothing but confusion had resulted

from the efforts at reform. To Kaunitz the confusion
was also apparent; but instead of regarding the steps
which had been taken as mistakes, he more justly considered them as half measures which had proved unsuccessful, but which called only for further completion.
With a firm grasp of the principle at issue, he therefore
produced, between the years 1758 and 1760, a scheme
with the avowed intention of advancing further on the
course already taken. When the "Directorium in
publicis et in cameralibus" had been established, the
object had been the proper connection of all the parts
with the whole, and the formation of a general system
for the administration of internal affairs. The object
had not been attained. The gradual establishment of
numerous superior courts immediately subordinated to
the empress had been entirely contrary to the avowed
principle. The effect was that each departmental chief
took care of his own particular branch of business only.
This weakness might have been cured by the appointment of a Prime Minister. But the composite character
of the Austrian Empire precluded the possibility of such
a solution, for no one man could be found sufficiently
instructed in the requirements of so many different
countries. Kaunitz therefore suggested the establishment of a Council of State, on whose advice the sovereign
should rest, while keeping in her own hands that power
which would otherwise have been delegated to a Prime
Minister. That the State Councillors should not be
departmental chiefs, was the one indispensable condition.
They should be men representing the existing noble ranks,
with special knowledge either of special parts of the
empire or of special departments, and should be charged

only with the duties of advice and supervision.   Of this
body the chancellor should be *ex officio* member.

The empress had already found in Kaunitz himself
a support on which to lean in foreign affairs: the Council
was to supply her with the same support in her internal
government.   She at once accepted the proposition, and
a State Council was called into existence.   As employment in the service of Government in any other capacity
was held to disqualify for the post of State Councillor,
there was some difficulty in selecting the first members.
Many of those best fitted for the work were ineligible,
and preferred to retain the places they already held.
The most important members of the first Council were
Haugwitz, whose Directorium it practically superseded,
Daun, who was especially charged with the supervision
of military affairs, and Blumegen; while, as representatives of the order of knights, two well-tried and useful
officials, Stupan and Borié, were selected.   The reorganisation was carried somewhat further, and each kingdom
and province was subordinated to a single chief.   This
change was not carried out without grave opposition,
especially in Bohemia, where it was regarded as a fresh
assault upon the power of the Estates; and an earnest
endeavour was made by the Bohemian nobles to place
the government of their country upon its old footing.
The indignant letter by which Kaunitz encouraged the
empress to put an end to this intrigue is interesting as
showing his sympathy with that conception of monarchy,
as resting upon a broad and democratic basis, which
subsequently formed so prominent a part of the political
creed of Joseph.   " Other sovereigns," wrote Kaunitz
in this letter, " are seeking to restrict the power of

the nobility, because the true strength of a country lies in the majority—that is, in the common people. It is to them that the greatest respect is due, and it is they who are oppressed in Bohemia more than elsewhere. Instead, therefore, of thinking of any means to get rid of this evil, your Majesty is being advised by your own servants to sanction a form of government which will only increase the evil, and which is in direct opposition to the sovereign power."

If the civil administration had broken down under the pressure of the war, the defects of the military administration had become even more obvious, and in 1762 a complete reform was carried out in the war department. For twenty-three years it had been under the presidency of Count Joseph Harrach, assisted by General Neiperg. Its constitution had been civil and not military. For years it had been obvious that Harrach, who was now eighty-four years of age, was entirely unable to fulfil the duties of his office. But with her characteristic dislike to remove her old servants or to injure the interests of a great noble, Maria Theresa had suffered him to linger on in his office, in spite of his well-known incompetence. Even her forbearance, however, had an end, and she found herself compelled to substitute in his place Field-Marshal Daun, who, whatever his weakness in the field may have been, was admirably fitted to supervise the organisation of the army. Under his presidency the Council entirely changed its character. The places on the board were filled by important generals, and the slow and often ignorant management of the civil officials was removed.

The Archduke Joseph was constantly present at the

discussions of the State Council. Though he was not as
yet, to external appearance, very eagerly busied with
his public duties, the greatest care was taken for
his instruction. Men of the widest experience and
knowledge were employed, each in their particular
sphere, to write, for his benefit, accounts both political
and statistical of the various parts of the Empire. How
far he read them is by no means certain, but under his
apparent carelessness there is evident proof in the
memorials he occasionally wrote, and laid before the
empress, that his mind was already deeply engaged with
the problems of government, and that, as he expressed
it in a paper written about this time, he was "fully
convinced of the necessity of some form of despotism."
It is upon him that interest centres immediately after
the peace.

Scarcely had the Treaty of Hubertsburg been signed
when Kaunitz suggested to the empress that the time
had now arrived for the election of the Archduke Joseph
as King of the Romans, a suggestion which some years
earlier had been made in vain. He felt that it would
be wise to take advantage of the present moment to
re-establish the somewhat shaken position of the Austrian
House. As far as Joseph himself was concerned, it was
a sorrowful time. His marriage with Isabella of Parma
had proved a source of the greatest happiness to him.
She was a woman of unusual gifts. Her education and
her acquirements would have been thought remarkable
in an able young man. Her own description of herself
speaks, though in somewhat playful terms, to her many-
sidedness. Writing to her sister-in-law and bosom friend
the Archduchess Christina, she says that her mind is

like her desk, the receptacle of everything that comes to
hand : "a little philosophy, a little morals, deep reflections, playful songs, history, physics, logic, novels,
metaphysics, and a constant longing for you." Joseph
had found in her all he needed.   One strange peculiarity
she had, she seemed in love with death.   However much
she struggled to hide it, a fixed melancholy lay behind
all outward signs of cheerfulness.   She longed for the
hour when her life would cease, and believed that this
hour would soon come to her.   In this foreboding she
was not wrong, for in November 1763 she was attacked
by the small-pox, and died after an illness of five days,
in her twenty-first year.   The loss to her husband was
quite irreparable, nor did he ever recover from it ; the
remembrance of his early happiness never left him.   He
was still in the depths of his sorrow when he was called
upon to undergo the formidable ceremonial of his coronation at Frankfort.   For no difficulty had arisen to
prevent his election.   Prussia was pledged by the late
treaty, England and Hanover had always been eager
for his election.   The death of Augustus of Saxony,
followed almost immediately by the death of his son,
though rendering the assistance of Austria in securing
the throne of Poland to the Saxon House no longer
valuable, did not destroy the old friendship between the
two courts.   The ecclesiastical electors were easily won
over by a certain expenditure ; and promises of subsequent advantage removed the opposition of the Palatinate
and of Bavaria.   The election was, therefore, completed
with perfect unanimity.

Another step, which must have been most distressing
to Joseph, was taken at the same time ; on political

grounds, the necessity of a second marriage was urged upon him. He confessed the necessity, and expressed an eager desire to perpetuate the memory of his wife by marrying her sister, the Infanta Louise of Parma. But the marriage of princes had little to do with their personal wishes, especially in Austria, where experience had taught the value of carefully arranged matrimonial alliances, and where now the imperious will and cold-blooded policy of the chancellor was bent on re-establishing lost prestige and on maintaining the system he had created. Though their opinions did not often coincide, on this occasion the emperor strongly supported his views. The main object of Kaunitz was to knit indissolubly the Houses of Hapsburg and Bourbon ; but he was also eager to get rid of all rivalry on the part of the German princes, more especially on the part of Bavaria. As far as Italy was concerned, his great object was already secured ; for one of the archduchesses was contracted to the Spanish king's second son, now on the throne of Naples ; and one of the archdukes was to marry a Spanish princess, and to receive, as a second inheritance and separate from the Austrian throne, his father's Grand Duchy of Tuscany ; another of the archdukes was engaged to the grand-daughter of the Duke of Modena, and in due time was to rule in Milan over the united countries of Modena and Austrian Lombardy. Meanwhile, the Princess Louise of Parma, the object of Joseph's desires, had been contracted to the Prince of Asturias, the heir to the Spanish throne. In Germany, the position of the Austrian House was not so strong. Kaunitz, therefore, desired that Joseph's new wife, the subsequent empress, should be a German princess, and if possible a Bavarian. Maria Theresa is sometimes said to have lent herself to this view. In truth, however, although her husband, who had an abiding hatred to the House of Bourbon, was averse to any further connection with it, she listened with all a mother's sympathy to Joseph's earnest wishes. While recognising the political superiority of a German marriage, she used all her influence to procure for him the Infanta Louise. She even went so far as to ask the Spanish king to allow his son to resign his claim to his betrothed bride. Her pleading proved useless; and Joseph, finding his own wishes thus thwarted, gave up all personal interest in the question, and, though bitterly disappointed, placed himself unreservedly in the hands of his advisers. He was allowed, as a most unusual privilege, to see the two princesses suggested for him, Kunegunda of Saxony and Josepha of Bavaria. Both seem to have been equally unattractive; but having first seen and rejected Kunegunda, he expressed his willingness to accept Josepha. No marriage could have been more unfortunate. A very excellent and amiable woman, but without the slightest attractions, the love which she at once conceived for her husband was merely irksome to him, and added fuel to the deep feeling of disgust with which he regarded her. Outwardly he behaved with tolerable propriety, but he never hid from his intimates the aversion with which he regarded his wife, nor did he ever find it possible to show her any sign of affection. She did not however trouble him long; married in January 1765, she died in May 1767. But within a few months of her marriage she had become empress; and the brightness had gone out of the life of Maria Theresa, for Francis I. had died at Innsbruck on August 18, 1765.

There was one part of her dominions for which, from the very beginning of her reign, Maria Theresa had felt much affection and from which she had hoped to win love in return. She had always shown peculiar favour to the nobles of Hungary. They had filled some of the most important posts about the court, and had lived in intimate relations with her. As far as declarations went, she had been successful; the nobility as a whole had constantly declared their warm love for the crown and for the person of the empress. But beneath this surface of loyalty there lay, as ever, a tenacious clinging to their rights and privileges, which might at any time ripen into formidable opposition. The existence of Hungary, so separate in interest and so divided in customs and privileges from the other countries of the Austrian Empire, was contrary to all the new ideas of a centralised administration. Yet to bring it into line with the rest of her possessions was too impossible a thing for the empress to dream of. There were, however, certain points which struck her as peculiarly anomalous, and which she believed might be altered. Money and soldiers being the great require- ments of the time, it seemed unreasonable that one of the largest and wealthiest of her provinces should pay a contribution which was almost ridiculous as compared with the burdens laid on the hereditary dominions, and should supply an army which was of so irregular a character as to be useless unless combined with German troops. She therefore determined to summon the Diet. Taught by experience, she had since 1751 forborne to summon a meeting in which disagreeable quarrels seemed

inevitable. Her wants were however so pressing, and
her belief in the success of her conciliatory action so
strong, that in 1764 she resolved to risk the difficulty,
and to demand an increase of revenue, a reform in the
insurrectionary troops, and, as a dependent measure,
some amelioration of the condition of the tax-paying
and unrepresented people.   To pave the way for a
favourable reception of these demands, promises of
improved communications for the furtherance of trade
had been held out; the great nobles had been more
than usually flattered; and the order of St. Stephen,
the patron saint of Hungary, had been created and
largely filled with Hungarians.

It was therefore with good hope that the empress
betook herself to Presburg, amid all the signs of joyful
loyalty.   But no sooner were the demands made known
to the Diet than opposition was aroused.   As so often
happens when the crown and the people are at variance,
the real points were for a time carefully evaded, and the
struggle turned upon a trivial detail.   A certain book
had lately been written by Kollar, the custodian of the
court library in Vienna, in which the rights of the
crown in relation to the Church had been strongly
stated.   Among other things Kollar gave it as his
opinion that the crown was within its rights in de-
manding a money composition from Hungary instead
of the insurrectionary troops; personal service having
already been exchanged for the service of substitutes,
why should not substitutes, he asked, be exchanged for
a money payment?   The Diet believed that this book
was written with the knowledge of the empress and
for the express purpose of supporting her views.   The

nobles saw vindicated as a royal right the very thing
they had most dreaded in her former suggestions; their
freedom from taxation appeared to be threatened.   It
became a serious question with the empress whether
she ought to yield to the clamour.   At last she went
so far as to say that the sale of the book should be
stopped until further enquiry; beyond this she would
not commit herself.   But this incident practically decided
the line taken by the Diet.   The empress was obliged
to be content with a comparatively small addition to
the general contribution, to drop the question of the
insurrectionary troops, and to lay aside for the present
her designs for the amelioration of the condition of the
people.   During the earlier part of the sitting of the
Diet, she had shown herself very gracious, and had
visited the archbishop and several country houses of
the magnates.   The result of the deliberations wounded
her deeply, and she withdrew from Presburg with such
a feeling of resentment that never again did she summon
the Estates.   Her anger, as was not unusual with her
in its first access, drove her to write letters of extreme
sharpness to Louis Bathyany the Palatine and to the
Primate Barkoczy, on whom she had chiefly relied to
carry her propositions.   The deaths of both these nobles
following almost immediately were popularly believed to
have been accelerated by the sharpness of her words.

The business which met Maria Theresa on her return
from Hungary was of a more satisfactory character.   The
hour for the conclusion of one of the numerous marriages
by which the two Houses of Hapsburg and Bourbon were
to be connected had arrived.   The King of Spain declared his readiness to give his daughter Louisa to one

of the archdukes. The death of the Archduke Charles (who is said to have been his mother's favourite) had left but little choice; Leopold was to be the husband of the Spanish princess and the future ruler of Tuscany, for Joseph had resigned to him his claim to his father's inheritance. The marriage was to be celebrated at Innsbruck with every circumstance of splendour, and the young prince was to proceed at once to take possession of his duchy. Innsbruck had been chosen rather than Vienna, because it was feared that the bride might, amid the splendours of the capital, acquire a distaste for the comparatively quiet life of Florence. The Emperor Francis had much disliked this choice, but had not made any strong opposition. Leaving the Queen of the Romans and the younger children in Vienna, the rest of the family proceeded to the Tyrol. With due gaiety and ceremony the marriage had been completed, when on August 18 the emperor suddenly died. In the full strength of manhood, and accustomed to much bodily exercise, he had suffered from the confinement forced upon him by the ceremonious life at Innsbruck. He had also complained much of a feeling of oppression, caused as he believed by the close neighbourhood of the mountains which surround the city, and was looking forward to a speedy departure from it as the only means of regaining his health. His visit had almost reached its close when he was suddenly seized with giddiness as he was entering the theatre. Joseph, who was with him, assisted him to withdraw, but before he could walk through the corridor which separated the theatre from the palace, he fell to the ground. He was carried to a neighbouring

room, but never recovered consciousness, and in a few
hours breathed his last.

His death was a terrible blow to Maria Theresa.
For a while her mind seemed almost paralysed, and
the effects were of a lasting character. Her domestic
life was shattered, as many another woman's has been,
when the light and joy of her life passed out of it. It seems
almost impertinent to follow her in her sorrow. But,
in fact, it was her true woman's heart, underlying all her
political conduct and her imperial show, which made
her so lovable and interesting a person; and in her
sorrow her behaviour was intensely womanly. Though
her married life had been on the whole very happy,
though she had always devoted herself to her husband's
comfort in a way which is simply astonishing considering
all the work which rested on her, she now blamed
herself for a thousand fancied deficiencies. Though
she had long since discovered her own superiority and
the futility of her early hope that her husband would
be a strong support to her steps, she now pictured
him as he had seemed to her in her girlhood, and
never spoke of him but as a wise and great ruler.
She carried the outward expressions of her mourning
almost to excess; she cut off her hair, wore no jewels,
gave away her wardrobe, and lived ever after in
rooms draped with black or grey. She could at first
bear no signs of gaiety in those around her; even the
wearing of rouge was prohibited. She declared in the
first moments of her grief that she had done with
the world for ever, and would leave henceforward all
business to her son. A letter of instructions which,
according to her previous promise, she sent to her son

Leopold, is a curious revelation of the state of her
mind. No doubt she had intended it to be an instruction in the art of kingship ; it proved to be only minute
directions for an almost slavish exhibition of religion
and elaborate advice with respect to his health.

In her complete depression the empress turned with
full confidence to the one friend in whom she was certain
to find support, her chancellor Kaunitz. It is remarkable how entirely she had learnt to forget the absurdities
under which his great genius lay ; how immaterial to
her, in her firm and well-justified trust in his absolute
devotion to herself, were his vanity, his almost impertinent
familiarity, his cold haughtiness, and his little personal
tricks. In him she had long found the support which
her husband had failed to give her, and to him she now
looked for help both in her public and private affairs.
As she had always trusted him, she said, in matters
connected with her country, so now she must trust him
with the interests of her family ; and the two things
which she had most deeply at heart were the immediate
admission of her son to the rights of joint government
with herself, and the settlement of her numerous children.
She was not mistaken in her confidence. It is impossible
to read the correspondence which throughout the reign
passed between herself and Kaunitz without seeing that
the keynote of all his actions was his devotion to her
interests ; not merely the devotion of a minister to the
interests of his sovereign, but the strongest personal
determination to shield and support her in every part
of her life-work. The charge she now laid upon him
he quietly accepted ; yet it must have been with some
misgiving. In his heart the chancellor was well aware

of the difficulties of the position he would henceforward occupy, and must have contemplated the possibility of their proving too strong for him. Not only must he have recognised the essential differences in the characters of the empress and her son, and the hasty and masterful nature of Joseph's mind, but he already had proofs of their conflicting views in certain memorials that had been placed in his hands. In these writings, Joseph had explained his views of government, and had expressed opinions decidedly opposed to those of his mother; time and experience alone could show how far he would attempt to give them reality. Kaunitz could not but feel that to occupy the position of trusted minister, where the characters and opinions of the joint rulers were so divergent, might easily prove impossible; but in his devotion to his mistress he consented that the experiment should be made.

The arrangement proved in fact permanent. But before any lasting *modus vivendi* was reached, the experiment had to weather a series of storms which well-nigh wrecked it. Each of the three people concerned in turn found the plan almost unworkable. All the difficulties which Kaunitz had foreseen presented themselves, and his work became henceforward less satisfactory. He was continually reduced to compromises, and found his ability heavily taxed in so shaping his policy as to avoid an open breach between the empress and her son. His task was rendered the more difficult because in many points he agreed with Joseph. Hitherto his influence with the empress had been so great, and his power of self-restraint so strong, that he had generally been able to persuade her to adopt his views in their entirety, or by skilful modifications to secure at least the essential parts of his policy. The case was far more complicated when the plan he would have himself approved had already been the subject of controversy between the co-regents, and when his old friend came to him for sympathy and for assistance against the arguments of her son.

CHAPTER X

DOMESTIC AFFAIRS (*continued*)

1765-1770

ALMOST immediately after her return to Vienna, in September 1765, the empress conferred upon her son the position of co-regent. In her present state of depression, she probably believed that she would be able to lay upon Joseph's shoulders much of the weight of public business, and Kaunitz may not improbably have hoped that he would be practically saved from the difficult duty of serving two masters. The young emperor began at once to take an eager part in the government. His first measures already foretold the future direction of his policy. All useless expense was to be avoided. The great preserves of his father were destroyed, and the game, which had inflicted much injury upon the agricultural population, was killed off. The park, known as the Prater, in the immediate neighbourhood of Vienna, was thrown open to the public. And, by an act which bore all the appearance of self-denial, the condition of the finances was substantially improved; for he at once devoted

to the State the very great wealth he had acquired by
his father's will, and used it to carry to a successful
conclusion a plan for the conversion of the National
Debt, from five or six per cent, to four per cent securities.
He gave himself up largely to military affairs, which the
empress had especially entrusted to his care. Aided by
the ability of his friend Lacy, who had now replaced
Daun at the War Office, he busied himself with improving
the administration of the army. He undertook the
personal inspection of the frontier, and joined with
enthusiasm in the military manœuvres by which the
army was to be trained. He began to clamour for an
increase in the number of the troops, a demand which
inevitably carried with it an increase of taxation. He
did not confine himself to practical measures only.
He drew up a memorial, bitterly reprobating the existing system of government, and hinting, not obscurely,
at the necessity of a more complete despotism, or at
least a concentration of power in the head of the State.
This memorial also contained severe remarks upon the
current system of education, in which the prominence
given to religious practices was not spared. "Good
souls believe," he wrote, "that they have reached their
end and formed a great statesman when their son takes
his part in the mass, tells his beads, confesses every
fortnight, and reads nothing but what the narrow
understanding of his confessor authorises. Every one
joins in the chorus : What a charming young man ; how
well he has been brought up ! Yes, indeed, if our State
was a cloister and our neighbours were monks." It
would seem as if he must have read the letter which
the broken-hearted empress had sent to her son Leopold,

for the points he caricatured are almost exactly those on which she had there laid most stress.

It was impossible that either Maria Theresa or Kaunitz could approve of the line of conduct shadowed forth in these memorials, or of the tone in which they were expressed. The pressure of taxation had been already strained to the uttermost; and to Joseph's demand for increased contributions, and his assertions of the necessity for a larger army, Kaunitz replied in words showing broad and statesmanlike views. He pointed out that the equalisation of receipts and expenditure, good though it might be, might be purchased at too high a price; for the wealth of a country depended not on the amount of income taken by the State, but in the well-being of its inhabitants and the vigorous and thriving condition of its trade and manufactures. As for the army, it was, he said, impossible in time of peace to have sufficient troops to render all parts of the Empire entirely secure; a well-organised nucleus, with abundant power in the population to supply recruits when wanted, was better than a vast armament eating into the industry of the country and exciting the jealousy of neighbouring states.

But if Joseph's political views shocked the wisdom of the statesman, his language with respect to religion and education were even more offensive to his mother; it wounded her in her tenderest point, and seemed to throw ridicule on all that she held most sacred. The hope of practical retirement from the government, with which she had at first flattered herself, disappeared. With her eyes open to the dangers which might attend the inconsiderate action and bitter speech of her son, and with renewed interests in life as her sorrow slackened, she saw that the time for such a step had not arrived, and before long she resumed her full participation in public business.

It was now Joseph's turn to discover the difficulties of the co-regency. So thoroughly had the empress returned to her old position, that he found himself practically excluded from all exercise of power. The unreality of his position became unbearable to him. He refused to sign documents of which he did not approve, and demanded that he should at least be allowed to adopt some form of signature which should show that it carried with it no assertion of approval of the paper to which it was appended. The empress refused to listen to a plan which would have laid open to all the world the differences between herself and her son. It speaks well for the young emperor that he yielded the point. Indeed, his conduct to his mother was always affectionate and dutiful. He so thoroughly acknowledged her greatness and the value of her experience, that at this time of his life at all events, when persuasion proved useless he invariably yielded to her opinion.

This difficulty was scarcely smoothed when the chancellor seems to have lost heart, for he suddenly, on June 4, 1766, sent in his resignation. It is difficult to say how far he was influenced by the perplexities of his position, how far by dread of waning power.

A year which had brought to light not only the very vigorous character of the young emperor but the complete divergence of opinion between him and his mother was enough to make even the great minister

P

question his capacity for holding the balance between them. He was bound by every tie of gratitude, and indeed of affection, to side with his old mistress; yet he was too advanced a statesman not to feel considerable sympathy with Joseph's views, and too keen a judge of men not to acknowledge and admire the activity of his mind. It must have seemed to him an almost impossible task to harmonise the claims of affection and of political sympathy. He may well have thought that he had already fulfilled his duty, and that it would be wiser to leave to new and younger men the solution of the new problem that had arisen. But it is probable that he would not have despaired, had not other circumstances occurred by which his pride was touched. As he grew older some of his faults became exaggerated. The extreme and elaborate care with which each subject was discussed and brought into writing was degenerating into prolixity. His health, though he was never ill, was always weak; and he was beginning to spare himself more than in his youth. As a consequence, the work of the Chancery became slow, and often fell into arrears. This increasing tendency to delay did not escape the notice of the empress, and she sought for some means of curing the defect without hurting the feelings of her old friend. Stahremberg had been ambassador in Paris for many years, and had played a distinguished part in all the political questions of the day; it was time that he should be recalled and employed in the central administration. She therefore resolved to bring him home, to make him a member of the State Council and of the Conference, and allow him to do a large part of the work hitherto done by

Kaunitz. It was impossible that such a plan could be hidden from the chancellor. It seemed to him as if his position, already almost intolerable, was to be rendered still more difficult by the withdrawal of the full confidence of his imperial mistress. It happened that just at this time the death of two of the three heads of the Chancery occurred, and a reorganisation was necessary. Before completing it, Kaunitz requested to be allowed to lay a plan which he had thought out before the empress. The plan proved to be neither more nor less than an unconditional request to be allowed to resign all his offices. He desired, he said, to give up his place as Minister of the Conference, Minister of State, chief chancellor of the Court and State, and head of the departments of Italy and the Netherlands; and he urged the empress to transfer them *en bloc* to Prince Stahremberg.

Shocked and astonished at this unexpected step, Maria Theresa answered him in words of almost passionate friendship. Would he desert her at a moment such as this, when she had just succeeded in securing his influence over her son? What had become of his warm heart? had suspicion or envy taken possession of it? or was she herself to blame? If so, why had he not told her? He knew that she had always begged him to speak to her of her faults. She could not believe that his great heart could be poisoned by low-minded jealousy, or by the belief that she would listen to idle prattle. She had learnt in her sad life the fickleness of friends, but had always thought she had one on whom she could rely, and was restful and content. Let him judge of her disappointment. She entirely refused to accept his resignation, and promised never again to speak a word of reproach to him. Her anger was over. One condition alone she claimed, that, whenever a cloud of suspicion rose between them, he would speak direct to her on the subject, and listen to no one else. And then, in words full of covert flattery, she couples him and his work with herself, as the saviours of the Austrian State, saying that his health must be supported so that he may train others to carry on their work after her death. "Let us die with weapons in our hands. Such is the only permission and advice that your mistress and firm friend can give you."

Such pleading could not be resisted. With an expression of sorrow that any suspicion as to the firmness of his friendship should have arisen in her mind, Kaunitz withdrew his resignation. A fresh arrangement was set on foot, by which he was to become High Chancellor (a new office), and Stahremberg was to succeed him in the position which he had hitherto held. It was now Stahremberg's turn to object. Such a completely dual government, with entirely undefined responsibilities, would, he rightly pointed out, be full of inconveniences. Finally, therefore, it was decided that all should go on as before, except that Stahremberg and Pergen should be summoned to Vienna, made members of the Conference, and, without any direct office, take upon themselves the more laborious parts of the chancellor's duties. It was understood that by this means a successor would be fully trained to carry on the established system of policy. Kaunitz indeed insisted that he should be allowed to resign at the end of two years. This point it seemed, both to the empress and Joseph, better to pass over in silence, in the hope that circumstances would prevent any future resignation.

The discussion had one good effect. It drew from Joseph a strong assertion of his confidence in the chancellor, a feeling which had hitherto been somewhat questionable. Kaunitz was therefore able to continue his difficult work, with the assurance that he had the friendship of both the sovereigns with whom he was called upon to act.

The second point on which the wishes of Maria Theresa were set—the establishment of her numerous family—had meanwhile been going briskly forward. Her eldest and cleverest daughter, Marianne, had reached an age when marriage did not seem easy. She was therefore established with large endowments as the head of the Abbey which the empress had founded at Prague.

For her other daughters, however, Maria Theresa determined to find what she considered suitable husbands. She was by nature deeply sentimental; it is hardly too much to say that she was a confirmed match-maker; she always took the warmest interest in the love affairs of the ladies in her court. But she had at the same time a decided opinion that the members of the royal family must submit themselves to political necessity, and subordinate their wishes to State objects. With her elder children this had not been the case, and the results of allowing them some freedom of choice had been extremely successful. She had even allowed the destruction of a favourite political plan in order to secure for her son Joseph the wife he wanted; and after the death of his first wife she had interested herself warmly in his endeavour to perpetuate the happiness of his first marriage by continued connection with the House of Parma.

Her second daughter, Christina, was peculiarly dear to her, and for her also she allowed her natural feelings full play before the chancellor had obtained the right of interference. Isabella of Parma had from the first found a close friend in Christina; and in the certainty of her own early death she had been anxious that this well-loved sister should take the place she had herself held as the support and confidante of the empress. She had written her a letter, which, in the case of one so young, is most wonderful in its analysis of character, pointing out to her the means of overcoming the apparent coldness with which Maria Theresa treated her children. Her efforts had proved successful, and Christina had come very close to her mother's heart. The affections of the Archduchess were fixed upon the fourth son of Augustus III., Albert of Saxony, a young man whose character and great abilities had secured him a favourable position about the court. But there was an obstacle in the way of the marriage. For the Emperor Francis was very anxious to keep up the connection with Sardinia, and had fixed upon the Duke of Chablais as a fitting husband for Christina. In the last moments of his life, at the meeting of Innsbruck, he had insisted on the Duke's presence with a view to advancing the match. His sudden death having removed the obstacle, the empress was free to listen to the promptings of her own heart, and the marriage was celebrated with every sign of extraordinary favour. A lavish settlement was made upon the bride, and Albert

was shortly after appointed to the government of
Hungary. The empress had no cause to regret her
decision. A close and happy intimacy continued between
the mother and daughter. In Vienna and in her
country residences the empress set apart special rooms
for the use of Albert and his wife during their frequent
visits, while in their home at Presburg, within easy reach
of the capital, she always found a resting-place, where
she could shake off some of the trammels of ceremony, and
enjoy something of that domestic life from which her
great position generally debarred her.

In the case of her younger children, when sentiment
was banished and political objects became paramount,
the result of her matrimonial schemes was far less
satisfactory. Her daughters were sacrificed, one after the
other, to the great object of drawing closer her connection
with the Bourbon House. But, though she obtained
the political advantages at which she aimed, her motherly
heart must have been wrung with grief when her young
daughter Caroline, Queen of Naples, told her that the
early days of her marriage had been nothing short of
a hell upon earth, and when the misguided perversity
of another daughter, Amelia of Parma, compelled her to
break off all communication with her.

For many years a marriage had been contemplated
between one of the archduchesses and the Spanish king's
second son, Ferdinand of Naples. Josepha, the fifth
daughter of the empress, was the chosen bride. She
had been educated with a view to her future position,
and in their eagerness to complete the political connection, the parents arranged that the marriage should take
place in 1766, when the Neapolitan king had just

attained his legal majority at the age of sixteen, and his bride was a few months younger.

The plan, however, was for a while rudely interrupted. The smallpox, the terrible scourge of the time, as yet unmitigated by inoculation and unrestrained by vaccination, fell with sudden violence on the Imperial House and brought Maria Theresa herself to the verge of death. Early in May 1766, while the empress was still agitated by the news of the severe illness of her daughter Christina and the death of her new-born infant, she was told that her daughter-in-law Josepha had been suddenly taken ill. She had always been keenly alive to the sorrowful position of this lady, who had, in spite of a want of attractive qualities, won her esteem by the many solid excellences of her character; and she had done her best, by every mark of respect and affection, to make amends to her for her son's continual neglect. She now therefore at once hastened to the sick-room, to be with her while, according to the invariable medical practice of the day, she was blooded. While assisting to bare the arm of the invalid for the operation, she discovered the fatal spots which betrayed the nature of the illness. Although she felt a peculiar dread of the disease which had already more than once proved fatal in her family, she found courage to remain and comfort Josepha during the operation, and even to part from her with a motherly embrace, while with affectionate words she explained to her the necessity of complete isolation. It was a farewell caress. Five days later, the unfortunate princess, who had borne with much quiet dignity the disappointments and sorrows of her married life, passed away in an almost unnoticed death.

For the life of the great empress herself was then hanging in the balance. She had been taken ill after parting from Josepha, and now, on May 26, it was known that she was suffering from a virulent form of the dread disease. Loved and respected by all her people as few monarchs have been, her illness called forth the strongest exhibitions of loyalty. The streets were full of eager inquirers, the churches crowded with devoted worshippers; entertainments of all sorts ceased, and the gloom was universal. Meanwhile the empress lay expecting her end with perfect equanimity. She continued with unclouded intelligence to speak both of her domestic and political relations, and instructed her physicians to tell her at once when hope was over, so that she might receive the sacraments of the Church. The young emperor, who was certainly a devoted son, caused his bed to be placed in an adjoining room, and scarcely ever left her. He wrote, in a burst of feeling, to Kaunitz: "There is but one Maria Theresa, and I am more than ever filled with enthusiastic admiration for her." Khevenhüller relates how when it was thought necessary to bring to her the last sacrament, he met Joseph, fresh from his mother's room, who told him, with his eyes filled with tears, that she had just given him and the younger children her maternal blessing and last words of advice with a composure that was quite wonderful. Joseph was not alone in his devotion. Prince Albert of Saxony tore himself away from his wife, and in his eagerness forced his way, accompanying the sacrament, into the empress's presence. For four days hope was lost, but on June 5, Van Swieten announced that the immediate danger was over. An

intense feeling of relief spread over the city, and showed
itself in every form of ceremonial rejoicing. Once
begun, the recovery of the empress was rapid, but the
disease did not leave her scathless; she ever after bore
its marks, and lost much of her former comeliness.
On July 22 she was able to appear, surrounded by
her children, at a great and solemn Te Deum, to return thanks for her renewed health.

But the disease had not yet finished its work; it
attacked two other members of the imperial family.
Albert of Saxony suffered the penalty of his devotion;
but his strong constitution enabled him to resist the
assault. The young Archduchess Josepha was not so
fortunate. The distress which had fallen upon the
family had for a while postponed the arrangements for
the Neapolitan marriage. They were, however, shortly
renewed, and Josepha was preparing to start for Naples
on October 4, when she too was struck down with the
smallpox. The empress drew this advantage at least
from her late illness, that she was allowed to nurse her
child. But all her efforts were in vain, and on the 15th
the poor girl died. The tragedy is made darker, if it
be true, as was generally asserted, that she caught the
illness from a visit to her father's grave in the vault of
the Capuchin Church, a ceremony on which her mother
had insisted before she left the country. The young
Empress Josepha's coffin, the metal covering for which
had not yet been finished, was in the vault. Some
precautions were taken, but the young archduchess,
deeply affected by the scene, was said to have carried
home the seeds of the malady which killed her.

This series of misfortunes was not without one good

result.   Listening to the advice of her old-fashioned
physicians, the empress had hitherto followed the fatal
methods of the time which prescribed bleeding and the
total exclusion of fresh air from the sick-chamber.   Her
sad experience had proved the futility of these measures;
and henceforth both she and Joseph became strong
supporters of the new method of inoculation.   All her
remaining children and grandchildren underwent the
operation.   Having thus courageously set the example,
she became an eager advocate of the plan, and established
an hospital, to which she persuaded or almost obliged
those who were connected with her to send their
children.   Her measures met with complete success;
no further instance of the disease occurred in the royal
family; and in the whole empire there was a notable
relaxation of its fearful ravages.

The death of the Archduchess Josepha was not
allowed to interfere with the political marriage for
which she had been destined.   Almost immediately
after her death, the King of Spain demanded that one
of her sisters should take her place.   Maria Theresa
was at first inclined to choose her daughter Amelia.
But when both the Spanish king and Ferdinand himself
expressed a strong distaste to a marriage in which the
bride would be five years older than the husband, her
choice fell upon Caroline, who was then only fourteen
years of age.   It is strange that so wise a woman as
Maria Theresa should so lightly have suffered her
children to run the inevitable risks of extremely early
marriage.   No doubt she believed that, brought up as
they had been, she would still be able to direct their
conduct even when they had passed from her immediate

presence.   The marriage, which took place in April
1768, was not a happy one.   The character of Ferdinand
was indeed not likely to make it so, and Caroline herself
exhibited an amount of self-will which caused some
trouble to the Austrian court.   But she always remained true to her affection for her mother, and for her
younger sister Marie Antoinette, who was soon afterwards to become the wife of the Dauphin of France.

Before this disastrous consummation of the Bourbon
alliance was reached, another daughter had been sacrificed to the same policy.   In 1769 the Archduchess
Amelia was married to the young Duke of Parma.   In
this instance Maria Theresa is perhaps scarcely to be
blamed.   She was not acquainted with the personal
character of the young duke, and she knew that great
care had been taken to give him the best possible
education, for it had been entrusted to the well-known
French philosopher Condillac and his brother the Abbé
Mably.   Though Amelia had been dull and uninterest-
ing, she had always shown a gentle disposition, and her
mother had every reason to believe that she would
follow the good advice she gave her.   She recommended
her to avoid mixing in politics, not to attempt to change
the habits of her new home, and always to support De
Tillot, the minister to whom the late duke, Don Philip,
had entrusted the government.   It was a strange
awakening from this happy dream when Maria Theresa
realised that Duke Ferdinand was an illiterate boor,
whose sole pleasures were found in the rough joviality
of low company, and when, only a few months after
her arrival in Parma, the new duchess quarrelled with
De Tillot, made herself mistress of the government, and

insisted on ridiculous exaggerations of all the habits of the Austrian court.

The long series of alliances with the Bourbon House was to receive its finishing touch by a marriage securing to one of the archduchesses the throne of France itself. There was a moment during which it seemed not improbable that Elizabeth, the third daughter, for whom a husband had not yet been provided, would have become the wife of Louis XV. After the death of the French queen and of Madame de Pompadour, Choiseul was well aware that the king would inevitably fall under some female influence. A new mistress was at first contemplated, but the death of the dauphin had produced a certain impression upon the king; and his daughters, together with those members of the court who were shocked at the prevailing immorality, hoped that his reformation might be rendered permanent by a new and successful marriage. In this idea Choiseul participated. Always, in spite of temporary quarrels, true to the friendship of Austria, he directed the king's attention to the Archduchess Elizabeth, whose beauty had been much talked of, though in fact it had been greatly diminished by an attack of smallpox. He corresponded busily on the subject with the Austrian ambassadors in Paris, Stahremberg and his successor Mercy. But he was not alone in his comprehension of the king's character. The clique of courtiers who were bitterly opposed to Choiseul, fearing the increased influence which such a marriage would give him, found means to thwart the plan. The necessary woman was found, not in a wife, but in a mistress. The appearance of Madame du Barry at the court, and the king's infatuation for her, blew to the winds the hope of the royal reformation, and before long brought on the fall of the powerful minister; while at the same time all chance of the projected marriage came to an end, for Maria Theresa entirely refused to allow the negotiations to be continued.

But there was still pending another marriage project, which would not be affected by the king's immorality, and which would ultimately produce the same result as had been contemplated in the frustrated plan. The Archduchess Marie Antoinette, a girl not yet fifteen years of age, was engaged to the young dauphin. The marriage took place in 1770, after Choiseul, who had planned it, had been driven from office. It is difficult to understand how a woman of the robust sense and strong maternal feeling of Maria Theresa could have allowed a child of such tender years to be thrown into a position of such overwhelming difficulty as that which awaited Marie Antoinette. It is true that she took elaborate precautions to defend her from the dangers that surrounded her; that she kept up the warmest and closest correspondence with her, and placed the ambassador Mercy almost in the position of guardian. But it may be questioned whether this constant exertion of influence from abroad had not a disastrous effect upon the popularity of the princess, whether it was not, in fact, the origin of the cry against Austrian influence so fatally used against her subsequently. Nor is it certain that the advice lavished upon her was always wise, that it might not have been better to have left her conduct to the guidance of her own excellent judgment. And it is not without a feeling of regret that we find a mother, in most respects so noble and high-minded, insisting that her young daughter should recognise and even distinguish favourably a person of the character of Madame du Barry.   But in this, as in almost every other act which followed the death of the emperor, we probably see the fatal influence of her unquestioning trust in the judgment of her minister.   Kaunitz appears to have been both her good and her evil genius; her friend and stay, the accomplished executant of her best and noblest plans, her comforter in misfortune, her absolutely trustworthy friend; but, on the other side, a friend of so cold a temperament, so exclusively bent upon the greatness of his mistress, and with a conception of greatness so exclusively political, that his advice frequently destroyed or distorted those simple impulses of a large and noble nature, which often prove the surest guide to the highest form of success.

With the appointment of Joseph to the co-regency, the first and most prosperous period of the life of Maria Theresa closes.   The qualities which had won for her the love and admiration not only of her own people but of all Europe were henceforward somewhat clouded by the great sorrow which had fallen upon her.   Her splendid courage, the inexplicable charm exerted by the gracious vivacity of her presence, were blunted and veiled.   Her acute political insight remained to her; but its exercise was henceforward trammelled by the equally acute but less prudent opinion of her son.   She was still regarded by the people as the real sovereign; even the partial retirement in which she lived did not shake their trust.   But, in fact, the loyalty with which she submitted all questions of importance to the opinion of the young emperor, and the feeling of weakness in her widowed condition which urged her peremptorily to seek for his support, prevented her from exercising her strong will with the directness which had marked her earlier life. It is not in mere name that the subsequent years of her reign may be spoken of as the co-regency.

THE END